I0488132

The Stunning Sunsets

of

Door County

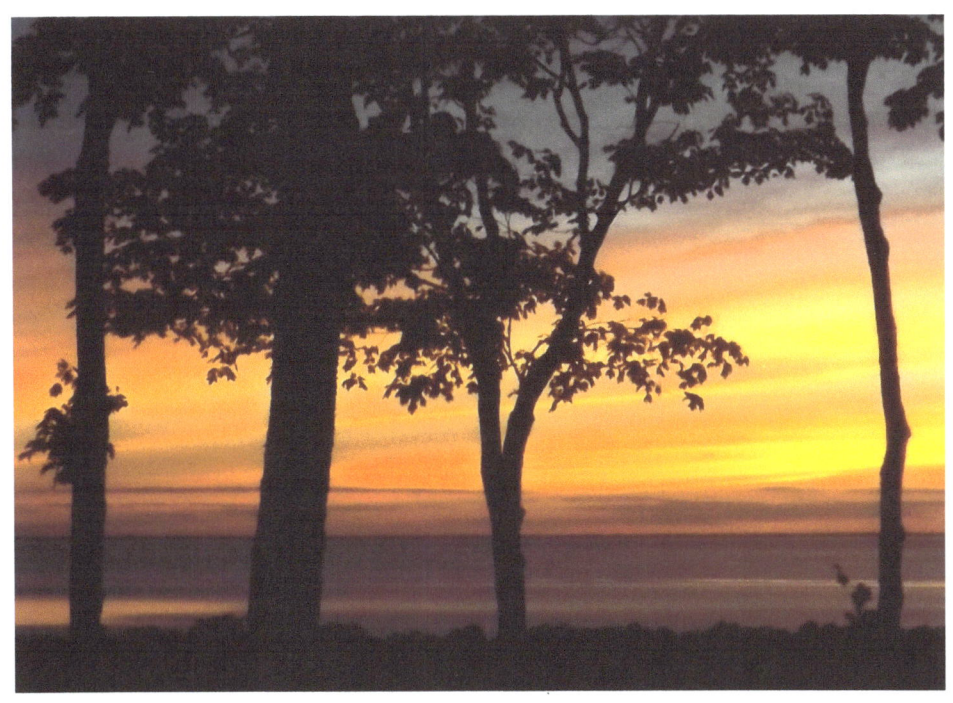

Deb Schense

Editing by: Deb Schense and Jeff Schense.
All photos by Deb Schense. Original fine art photography by Deb Schense. © 2014 Deb Schense.
All rights reserved.

Cover by: Deb Schense

Printed in the U.S.A.
ISBN: 978-1500679293

Contents

Preface

Several people had recommended visiting Door County, Wisconsin, as a vacation spot. We had ignored those suggestions for several years before researching the area further. A few years ago, we decided to take a chance on Door County and fell in love with the area. The pace of life was much slower. Nature's blessings abounded everywhere in the open expanses of water, forests, and hills. The boats, sailboats, yachts, lighthouses, wildlife, and landscapes drew us in. We loved visiting there.

Each day just before sunset, the world stopped. Friends and family found a bench or a westward view and people took the time to watch the kaleidoscope of colors that unfolded in the sunset. Once the sun had spent its glory, and the glow had disappeared as it sunk below the horizon, people wandered ever so slowly back to their vehicles, houses, or accommodations and settled in for the evening. The world began to turn again.

My family and I love the sunsets and wanted to share them with the rest of the world, so I decided to write a book about the sunsets of Door County, Wisconsin, in the Midwestern United States.

Autobiography

Deb Schense was born in Charles City, Iowa, and raised in rural Waverly, Iowa. Growing up on a hilltop farm, she learned to fish, horseback ride, and love the outdoors. As a young child, she would sit at her grandmother's kitchen table, color, and draw for hours. In her early teen years, she began to paint in oils.

Her favorite landscape oil painting was that of a barge floating down the Mississippi River from a vantage point at the top of a hill. After high school, she attended Kirkwood Community College and received an Associate of Applied Science degree. Later, she went on to the University of Iowa where she graduated with a Bachelor's of Business Administration in Management Information Systems. By combining her skills with computers and art, Deb now uses the camera and computer to create books and works of art.

She has worked with a small publishing company to produce many books over the past several years. Currently, she makes her home near North Liberty, Iowa, with her husband and son.

For more information on the books she has written, please visit: debschense.wix.com/bookem. To order prints, canvases, framed, or matted prints, please visit http://deb-schense.artistwebsites.com/. Titles of images in the book, match the images online. Greeting cards of any of the prints are also available. Contact the author for more information at debschense@gmail.com. All books, greeting cards, and prints are available with wholesale and retail pricing.

Ephraim and Ellison Bay Areas

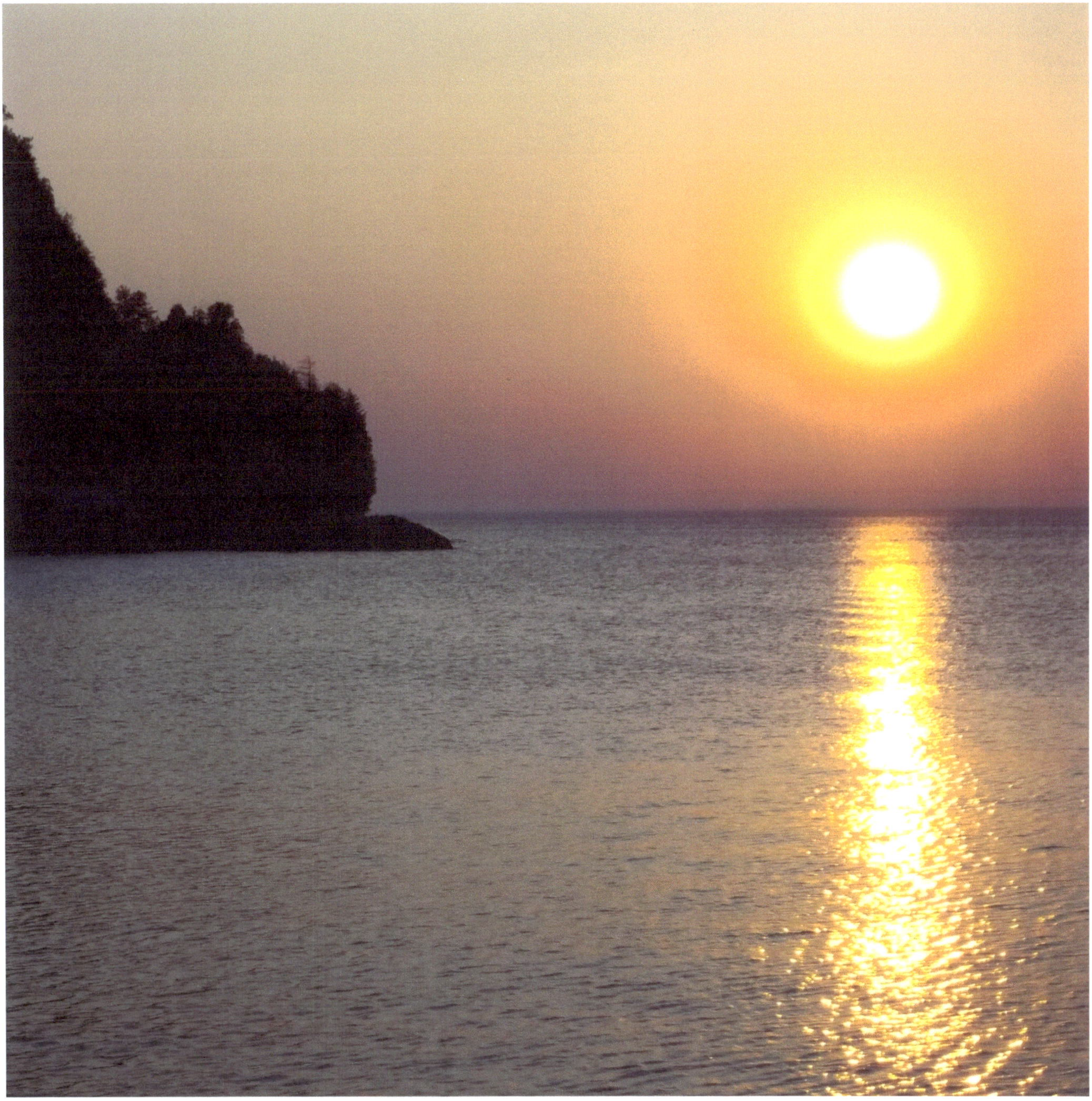

Bay Sunset

We started out on highway 42 in Door County, Wisconsin, one of the main north and south thoroughfares through the county. We would find a place to pull over and admire the sunset or take a short hike through the woods to the water's edge.

Ephraim is located on the west side of the northern part of the Door County peninsula. Door County is a place to stop and smell the roses. To admire all of nature, including the sunsets. Perhaps you haven't been there yet or perhaps you have. Now you can enjoy the sunsets in this book until you can travel there again.

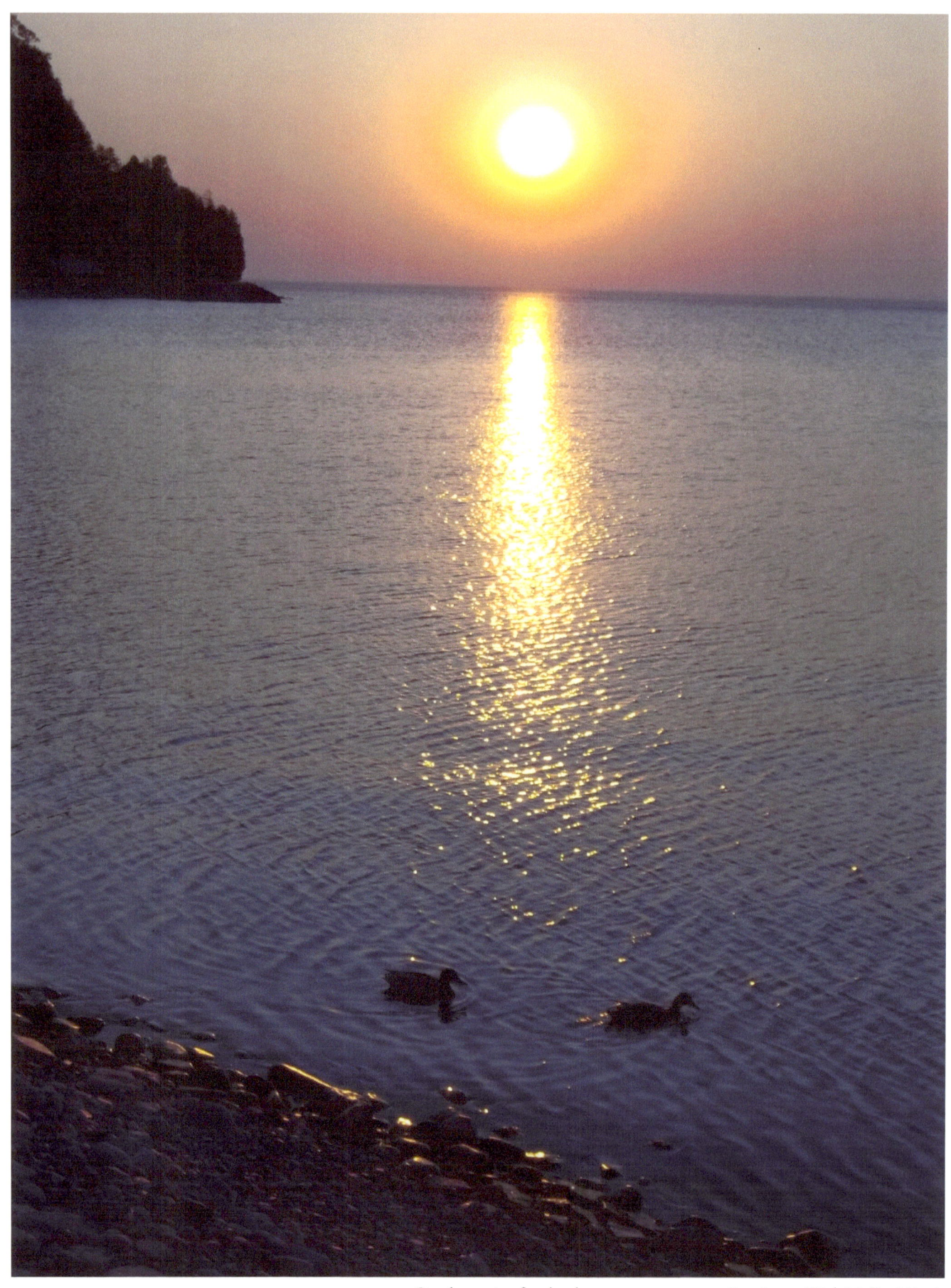

One last swim for the day.   *Bay Sunset With Mallard Ducks*

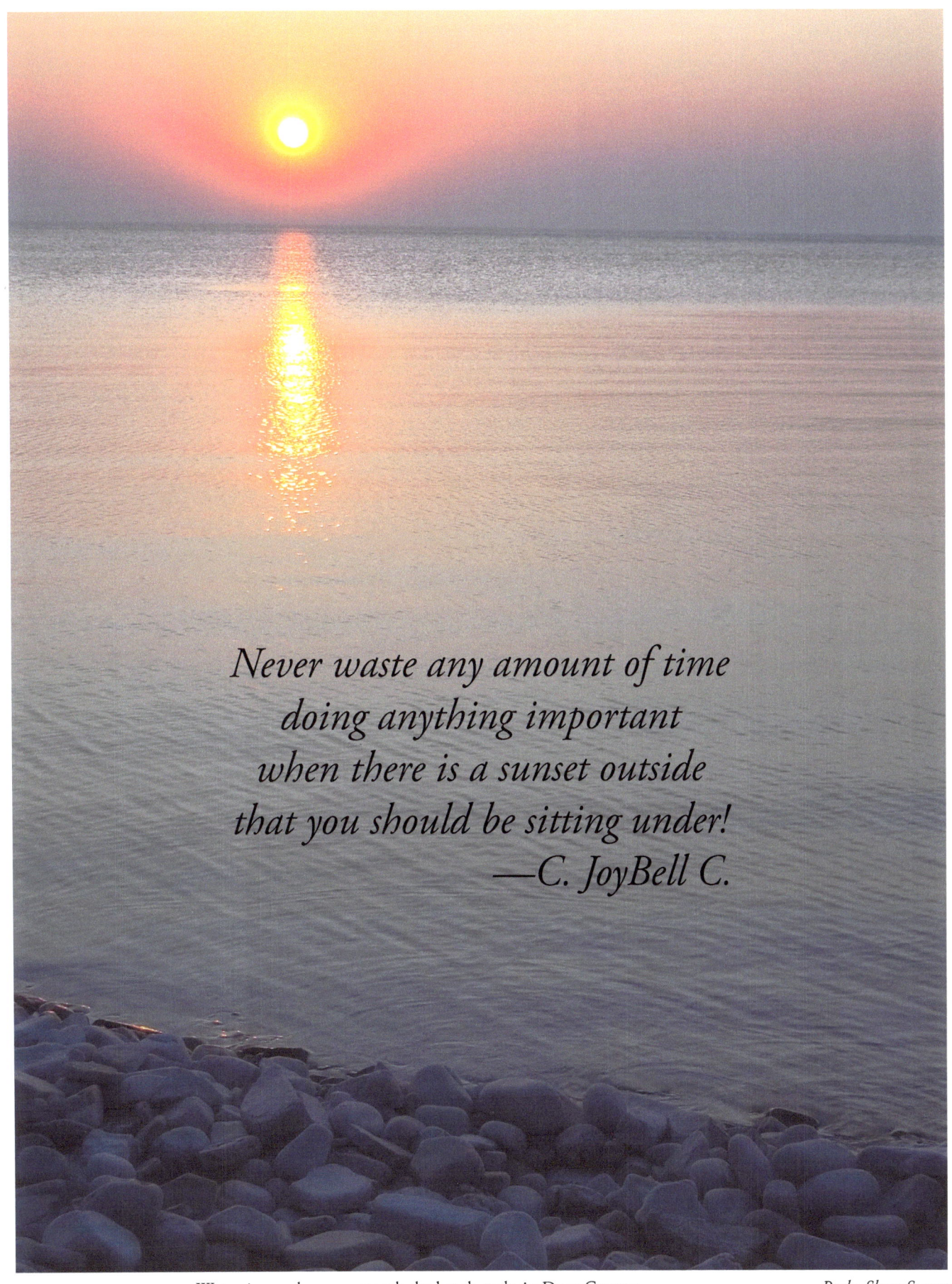

*Never waste any amount of time
doing anything important
when there is a sunset outside
that you should be sitting under!
—C. JoyBell C.*

Water, ice, and waves smooth the beach rocks in Door County.

Rocky Shore Sunset

Sister Bay

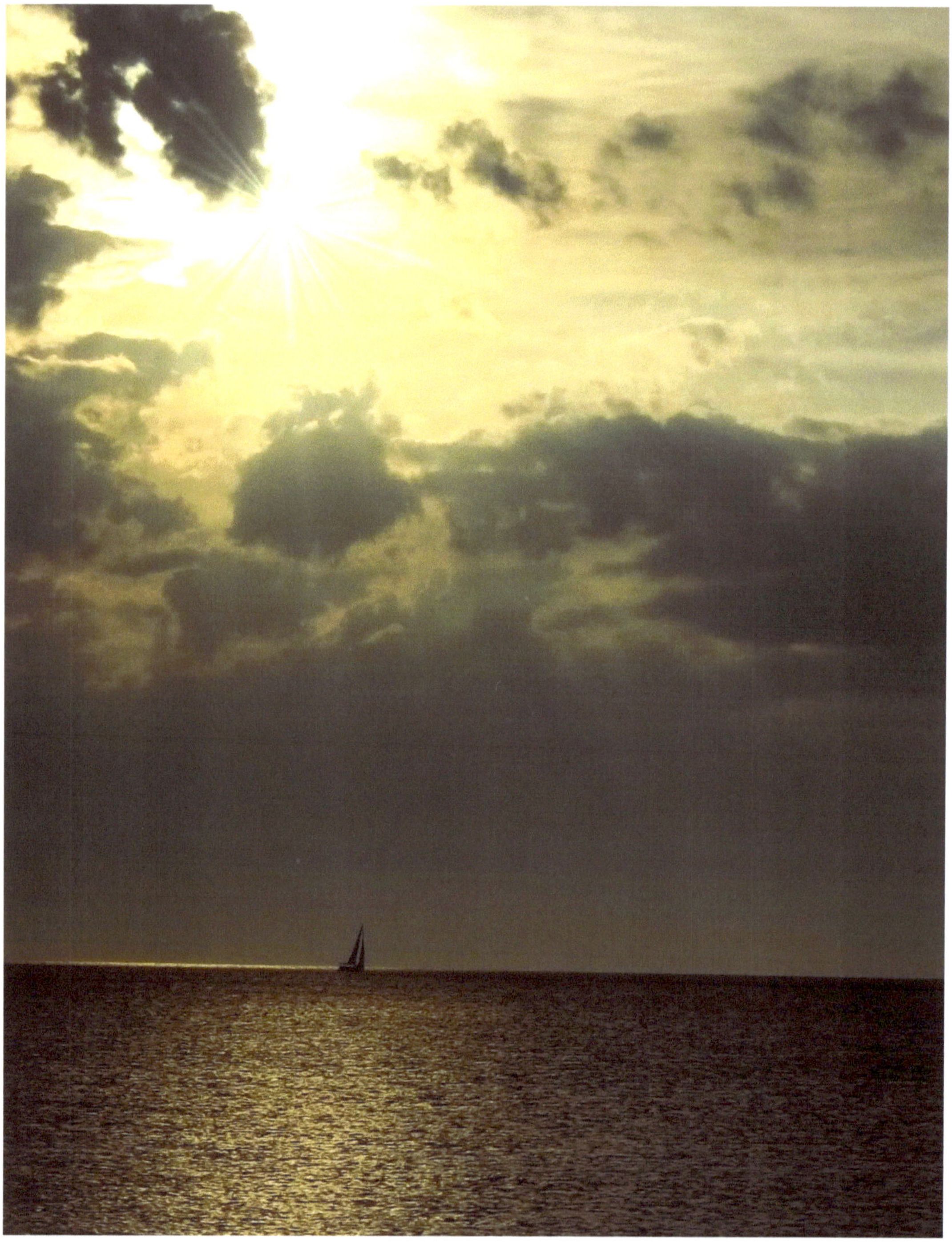

Sister Sunset Sails

Sunset sailboat cruises are available to leave your worries behind and enjoy the solitude and peace of the water, waves, and wind. Sister Bay, Wisconsin, is also on the Green Bay side of the peninsula and is the largest community north of Sturgeon Bay. The village was settled in 1857 by Norwegian immigrants. Al Johnson's Swedish restaurant currently hosts waitresses dressed in Scandinavian garb inside and goats on the grass roof outside. Be sure to check out their sunset and goat cameras on the web.

Artists find inspiration in picturesque shorelines and parks. A partial view of the town harbor is shown at right.

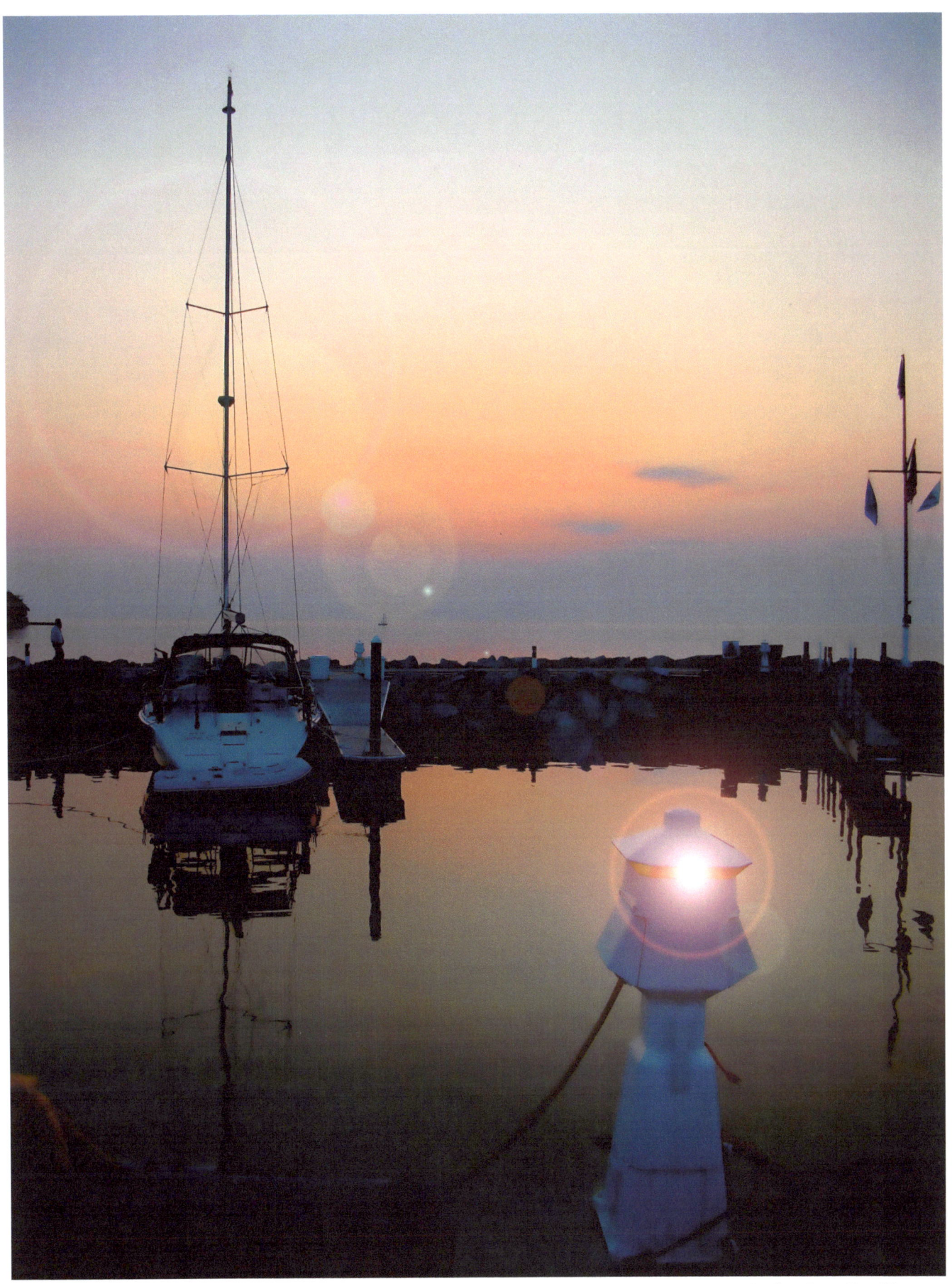

Dusk at Sister Bay, Wisconsin

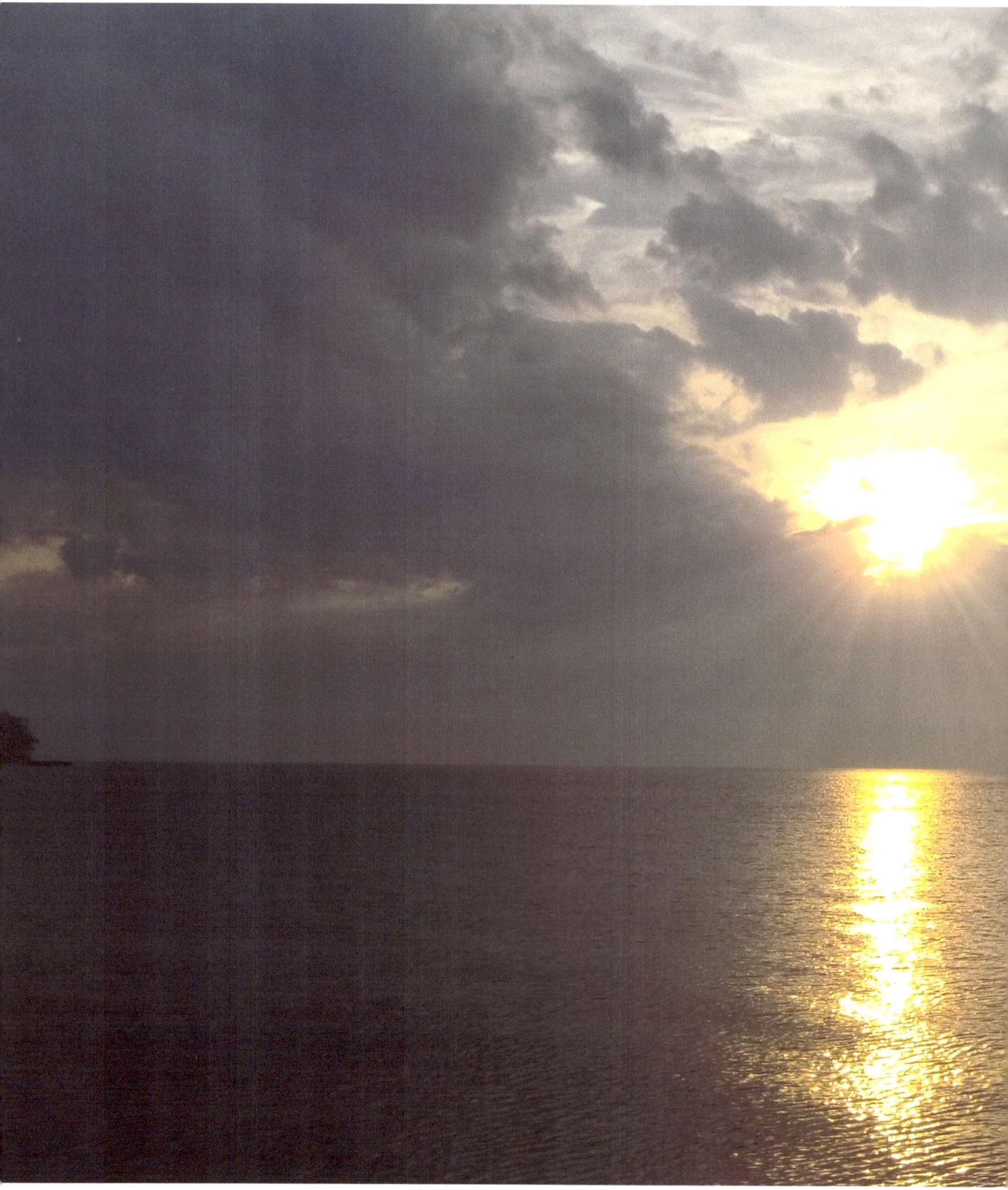

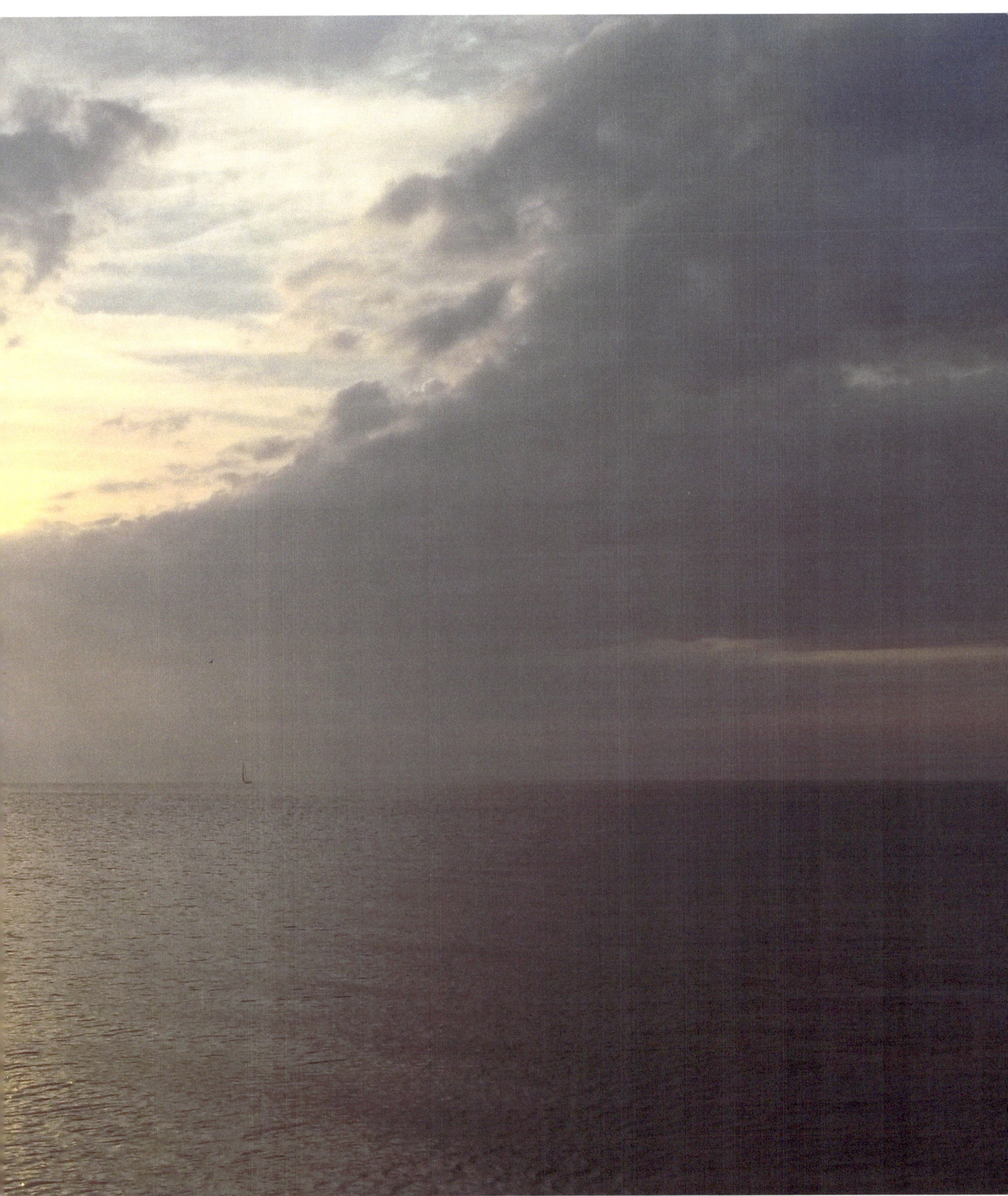

Sunset Sail with Sailboat v1

—7

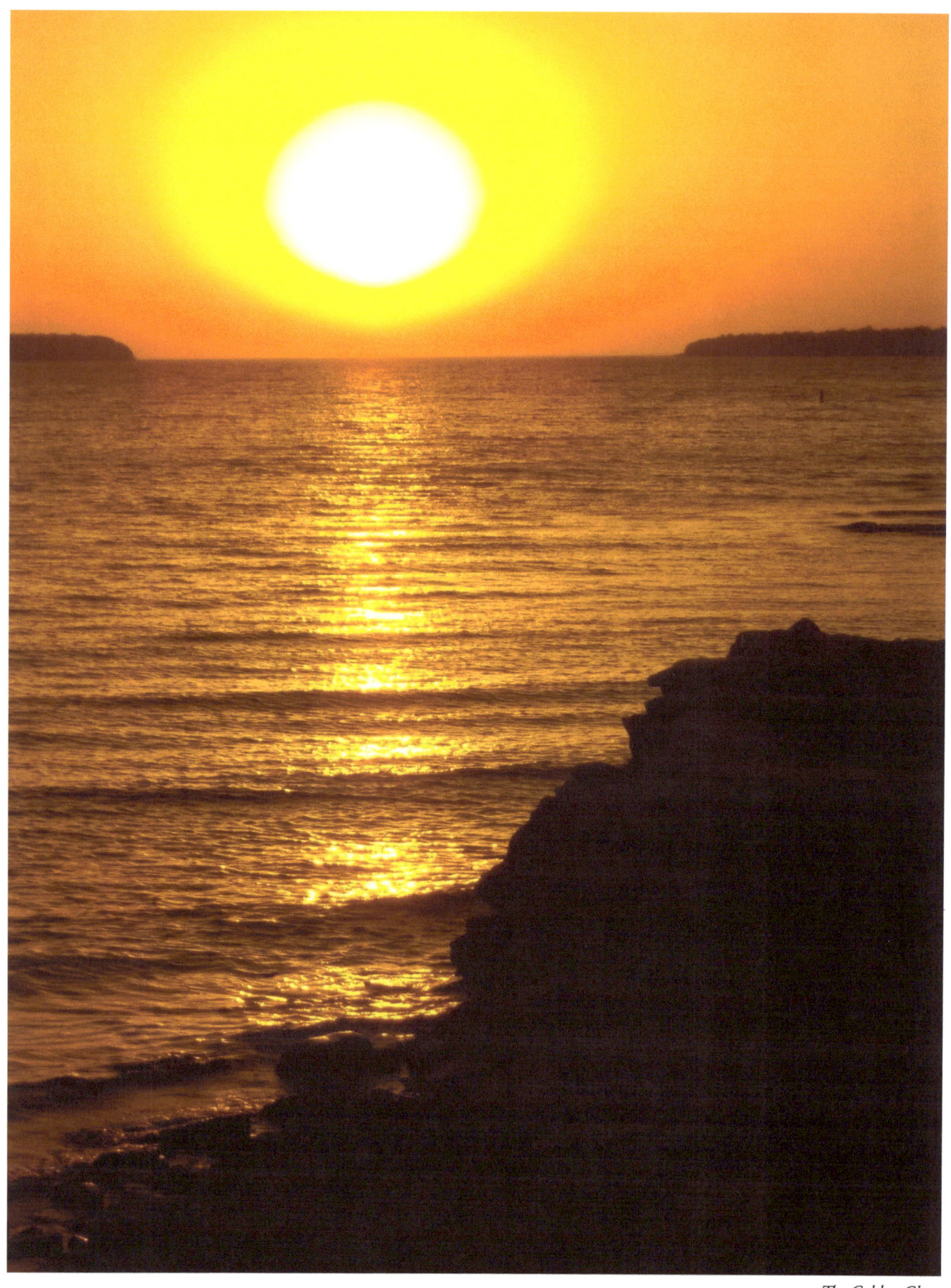

The Golden Glow

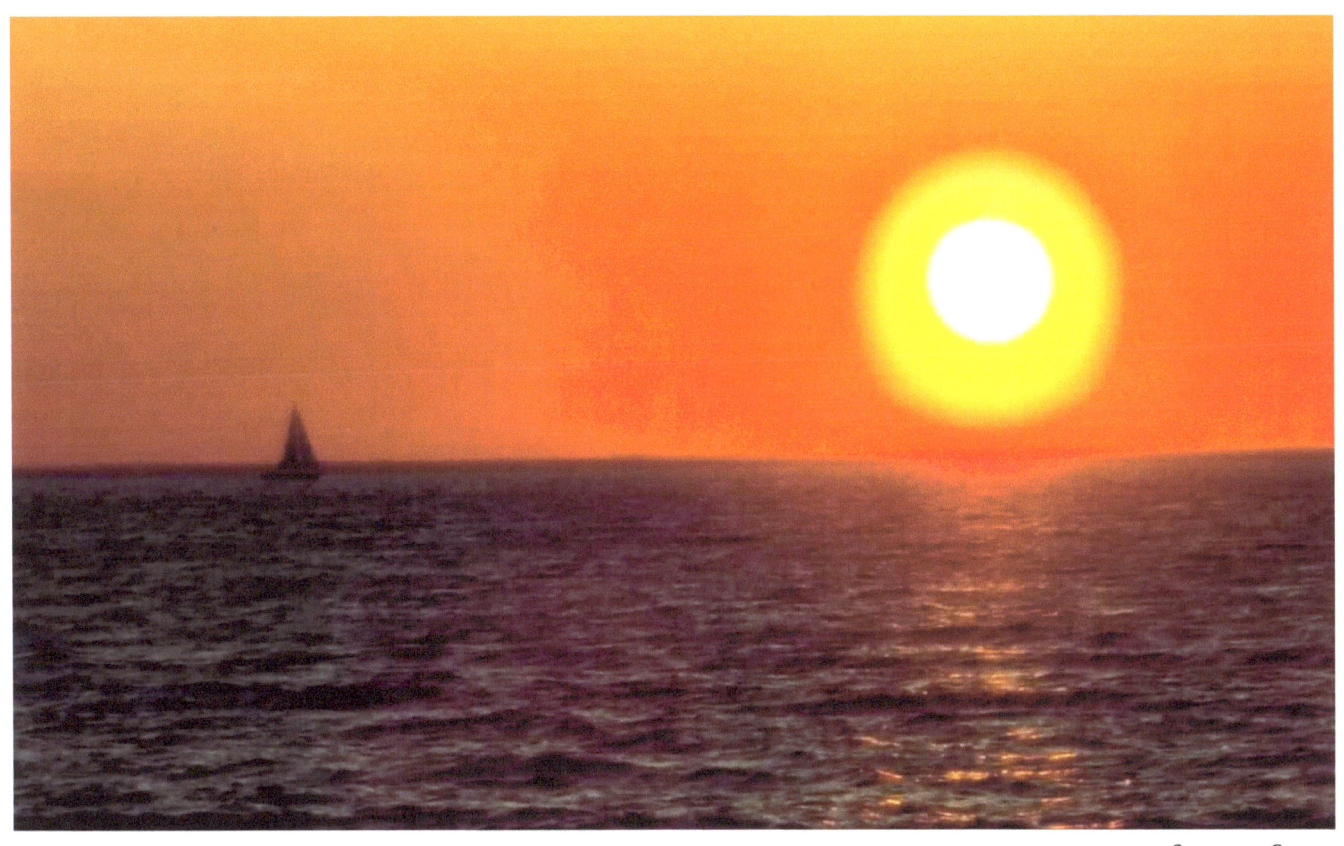

Sunset on Orange

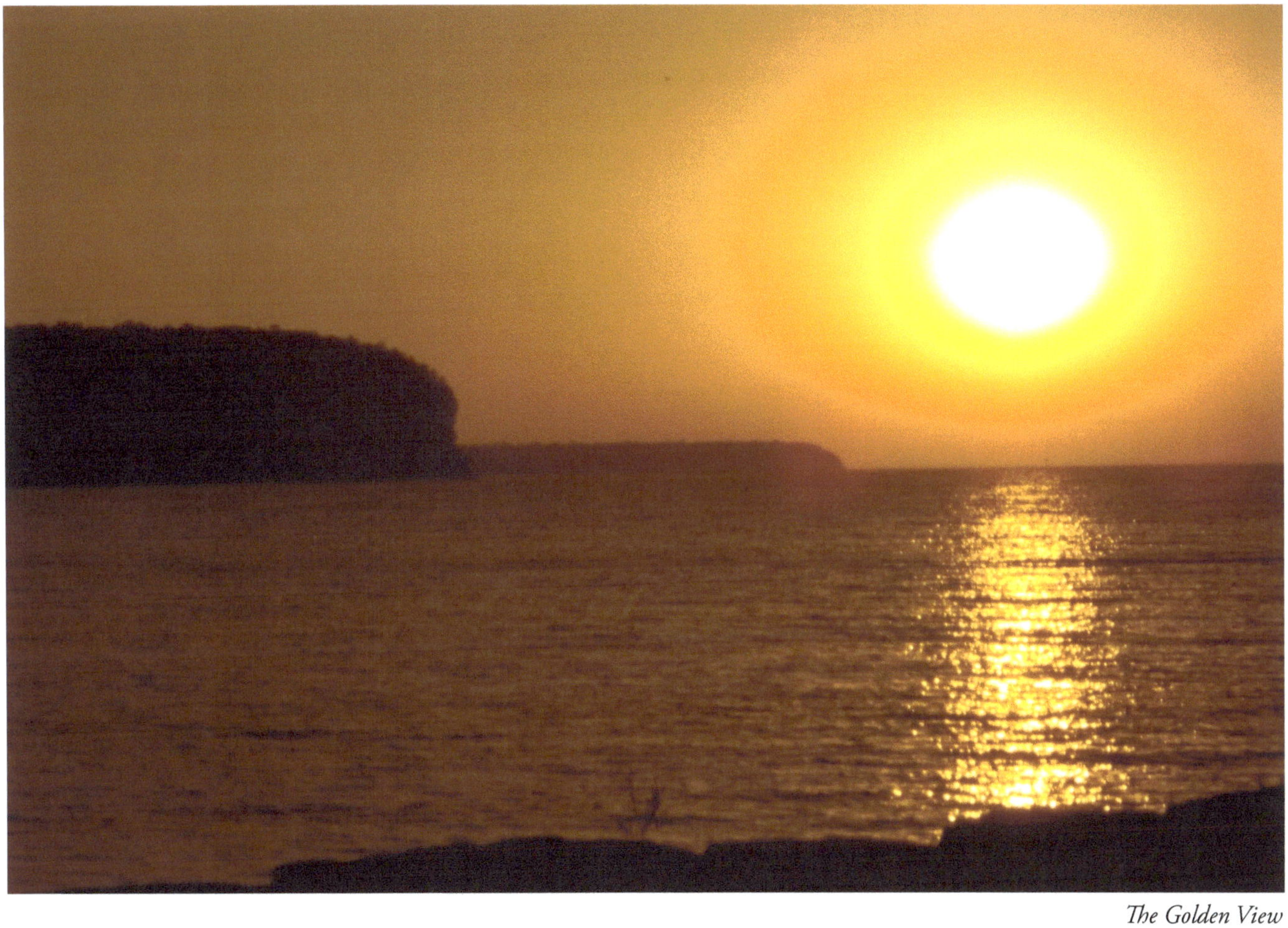

The Golden View

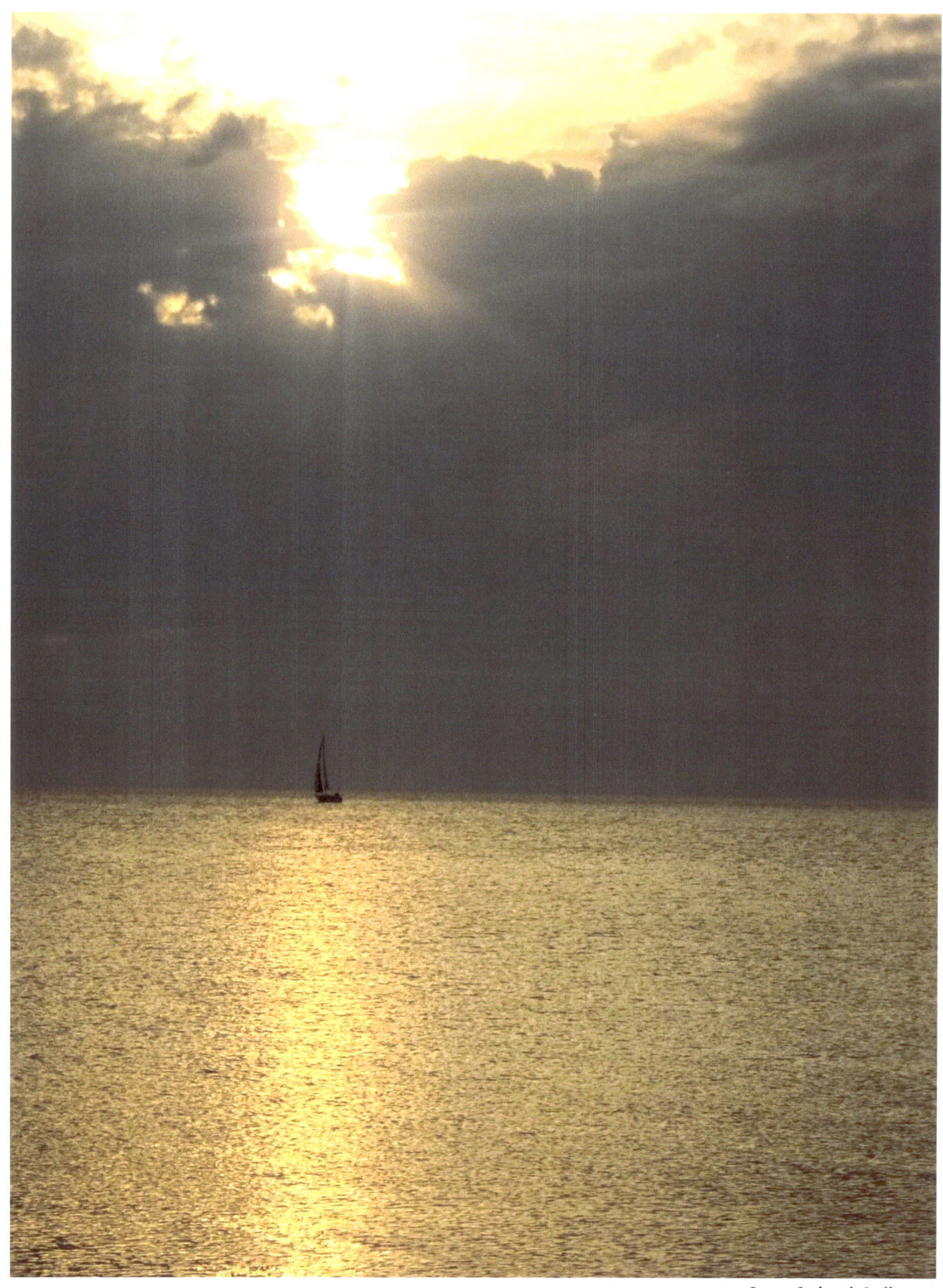

Sunset Sail with Sailboat v3

Egg Harbor

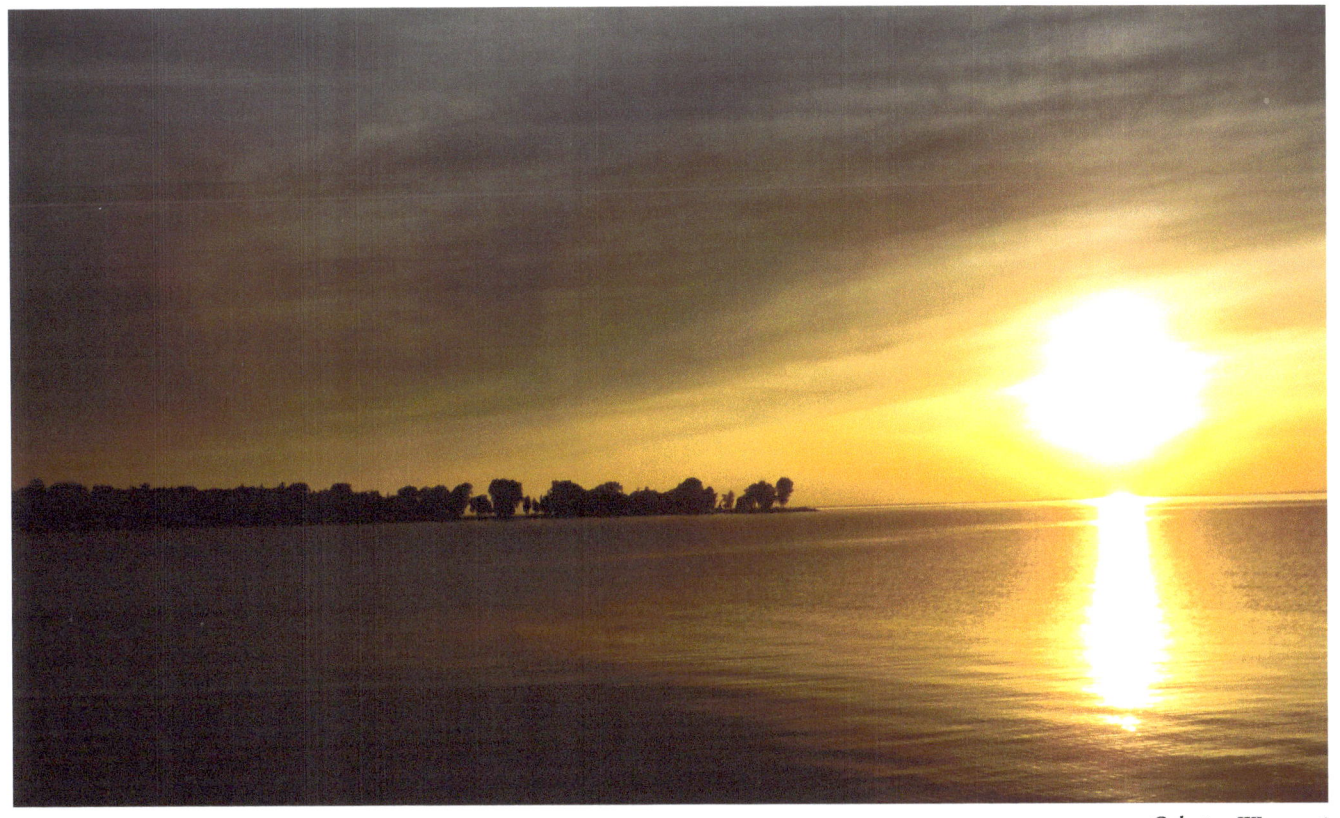

Calming Waters v1

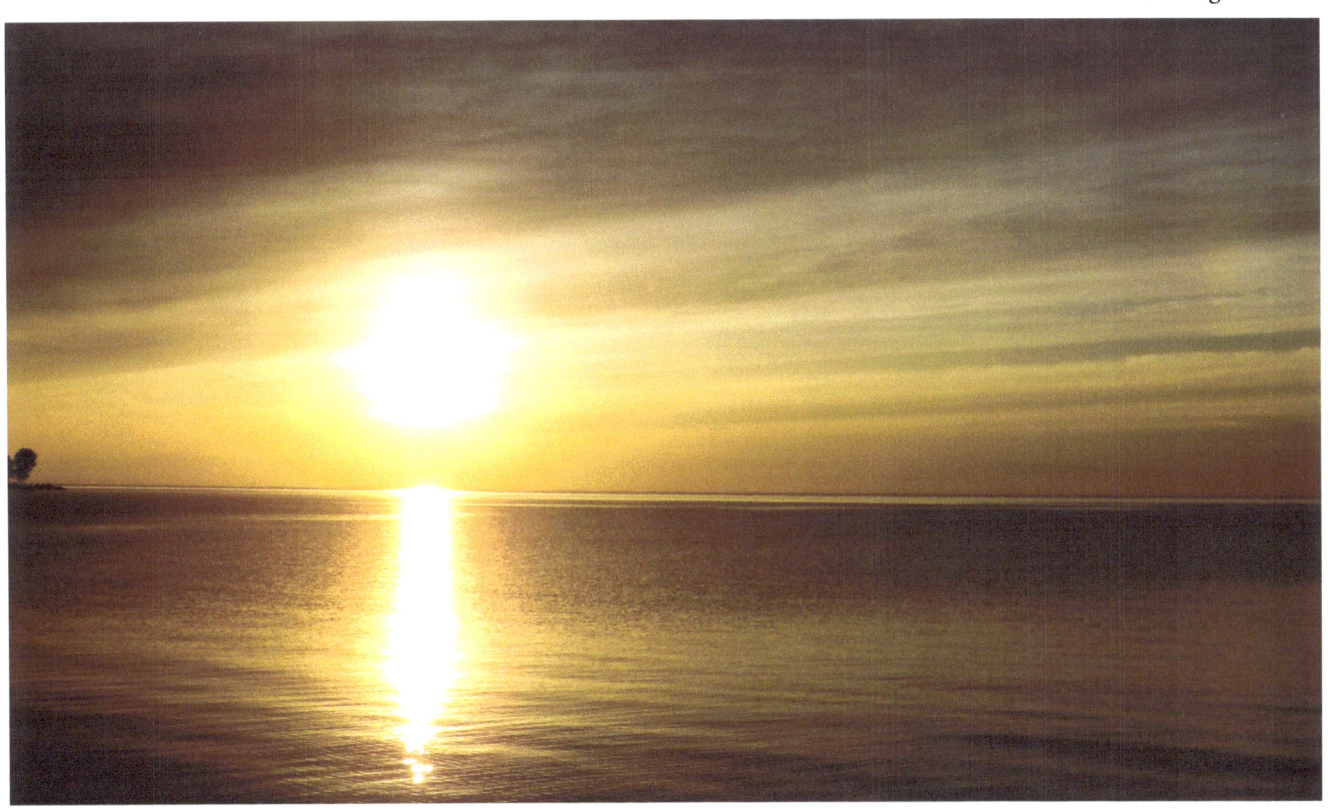

Calming Waters v2

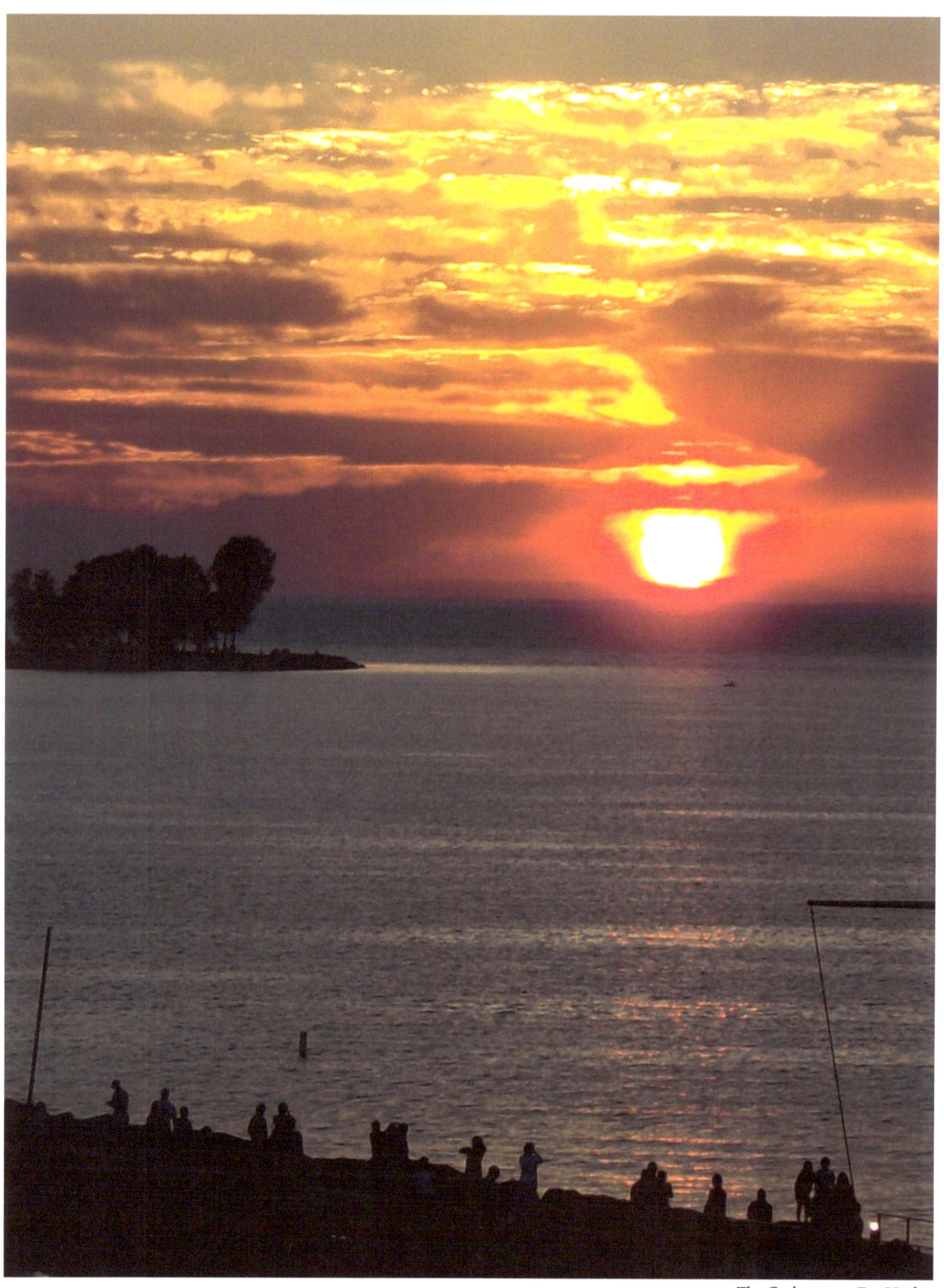

The Gathering at Egg Harbor

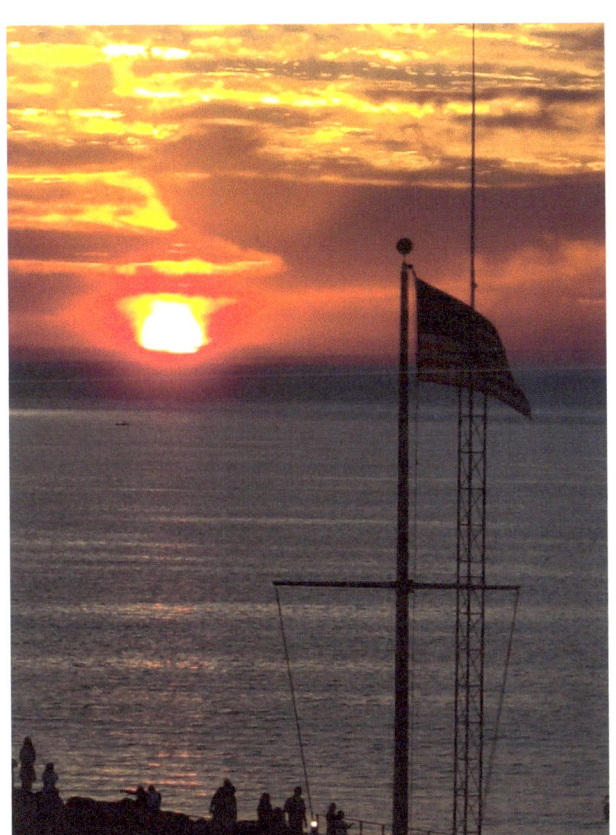

Egg Harbor is the county seat for Door County. It was established in 1860. Egg Harbor offers water recreation, walking trails, wonderful scenery, concerts, public art, retail shops, restaurants, and accommodations for visitors.

Year-round population is approximately 250 with temporary seasonal residents in the summer around 2,500.

In the last couple of years the village has rebuilt their marina, improved the beach, and renovated the Harbor View Park. The huge granite boulders are visible in the photographs on the following pages.

Egg Harbor provides many restaurants, pubs, shops, galleries, and an excellent market and an organic grocery store.

Within a few miles of the village you can find farm markets, golf courses, and wineries. The next largest city, Sturgeon Bay, is approximately thirteen miles.

Cherries have been prevalent in the village for over 150 years. Other industries include apples, lumber, and fishing.

The following photos were taken in and around the harbor area.

The Gathering at Egg Harbor with Flag

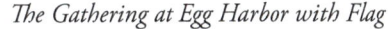

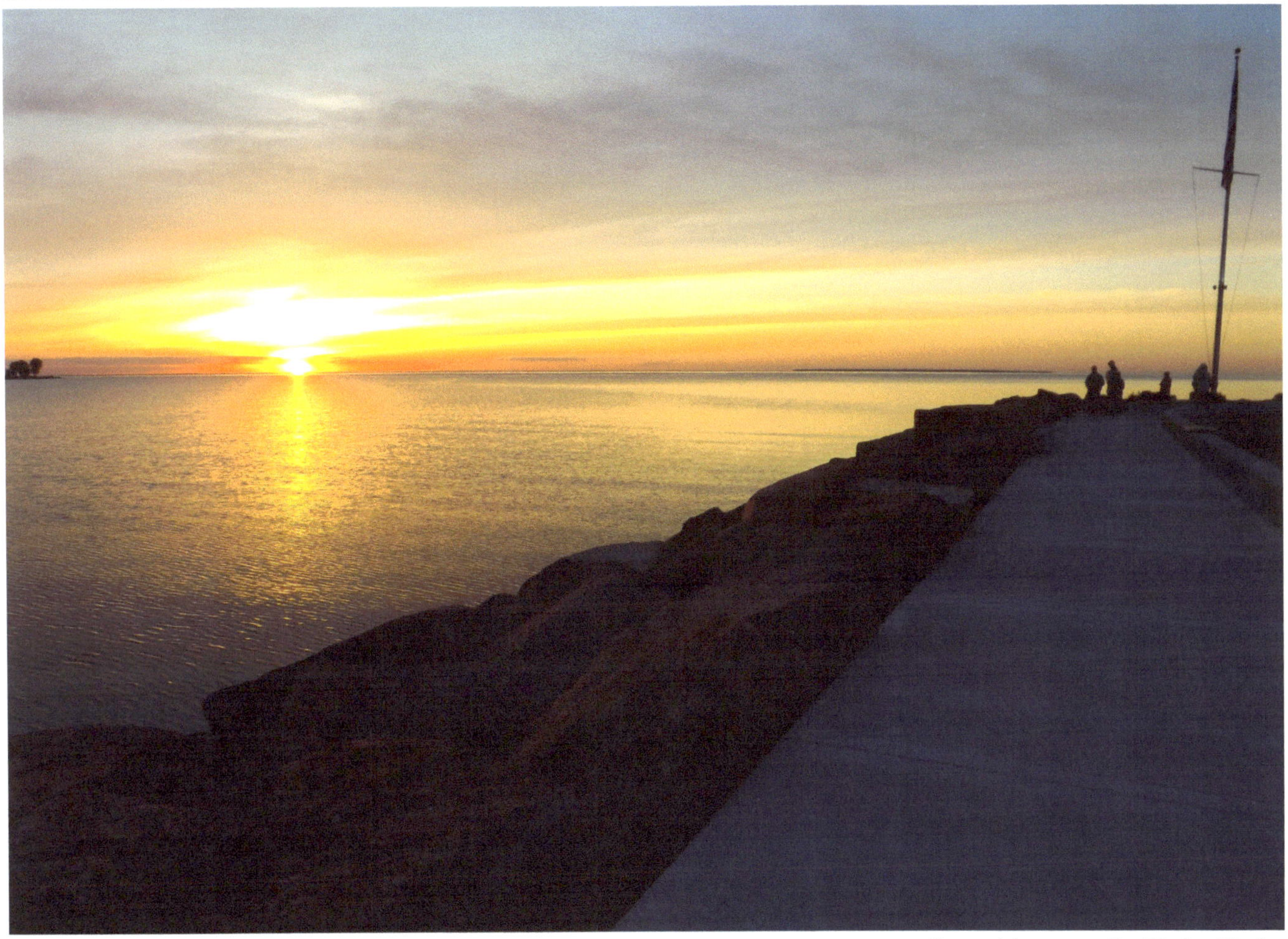

Sunset Admirers at Egg Harbor Harbor

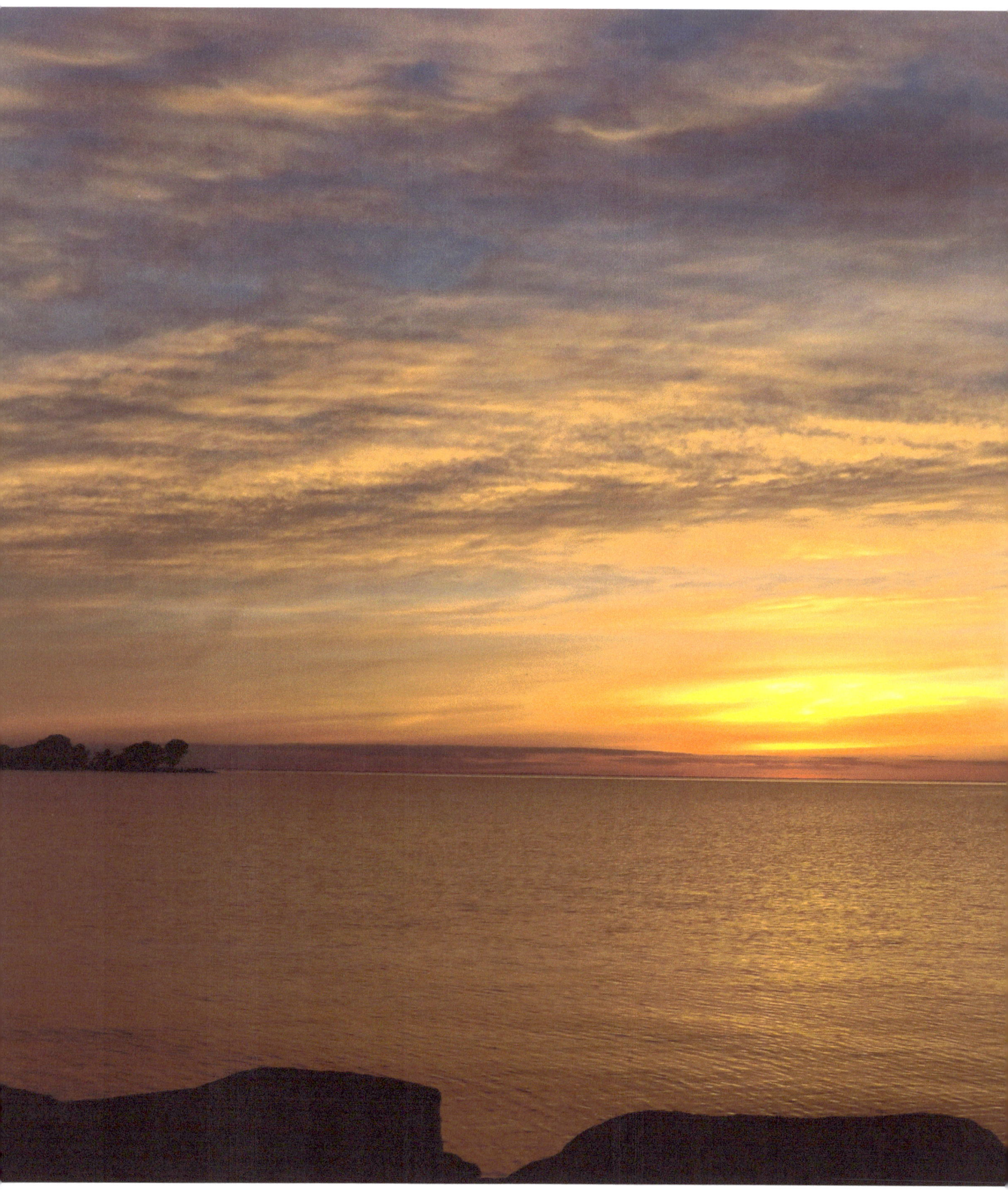

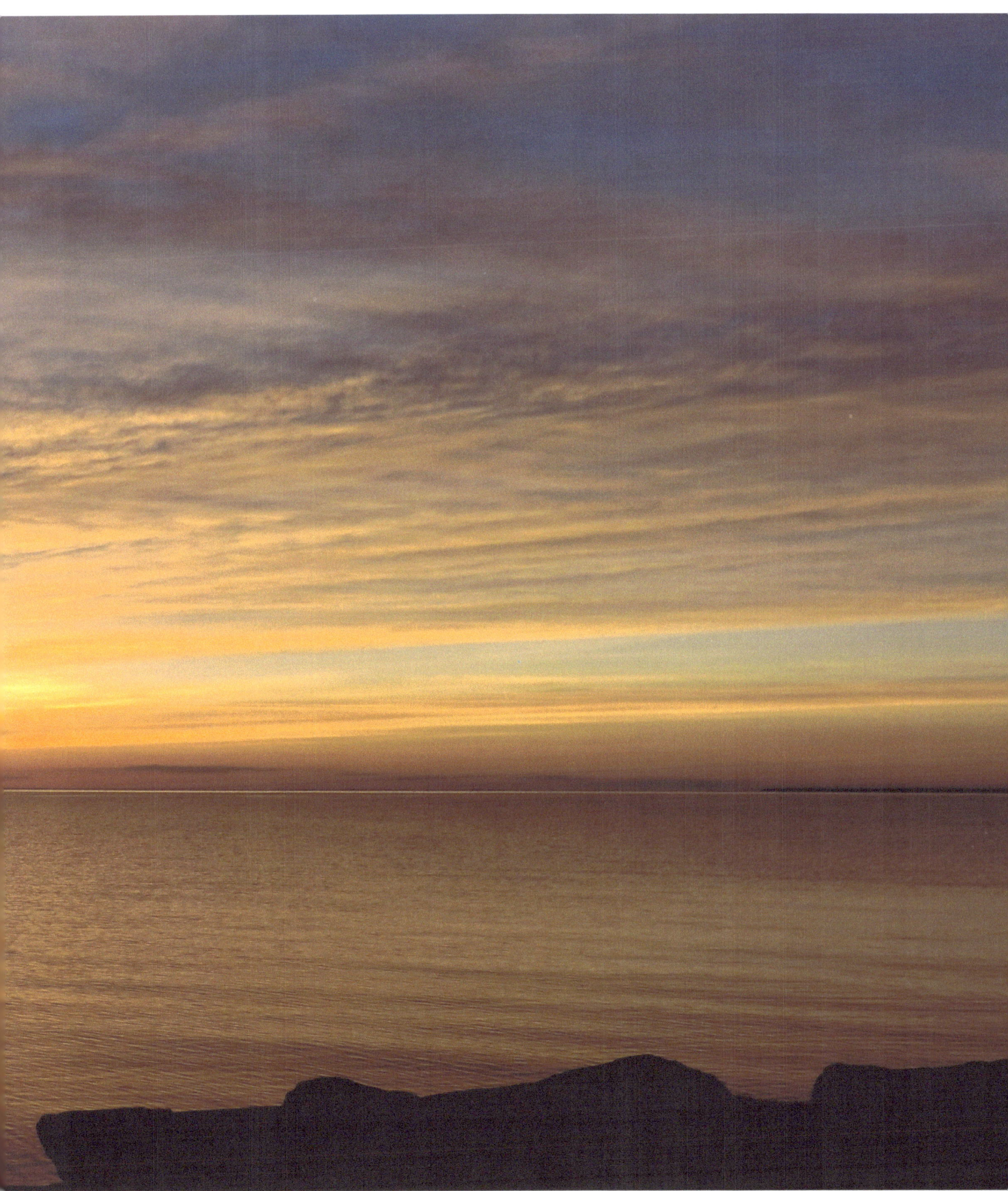

Granite Boulders Sunset at Egg Harbor Marina

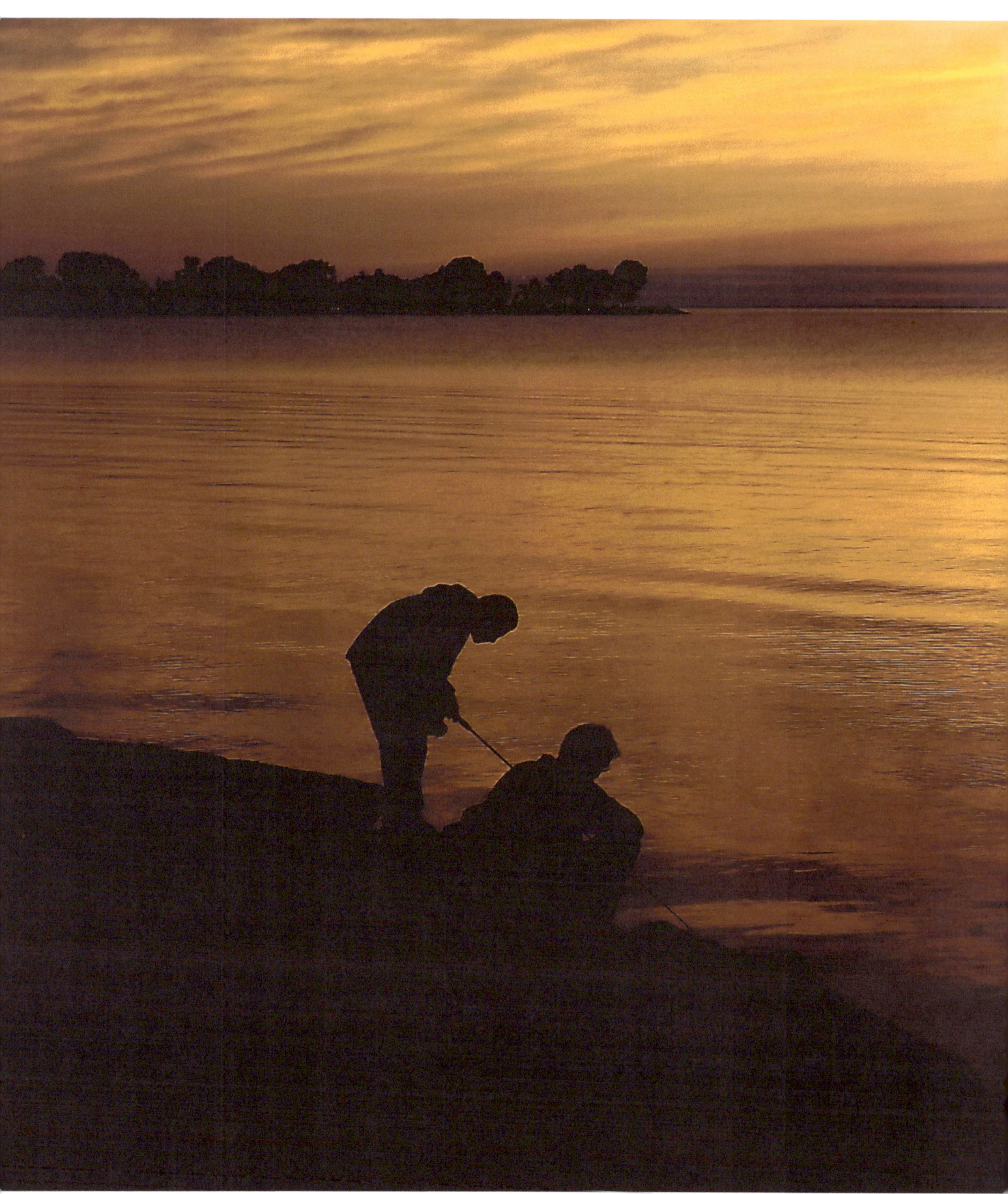

These two gentlemen are hoping for one more fish before sunset. They didn't want to give up.

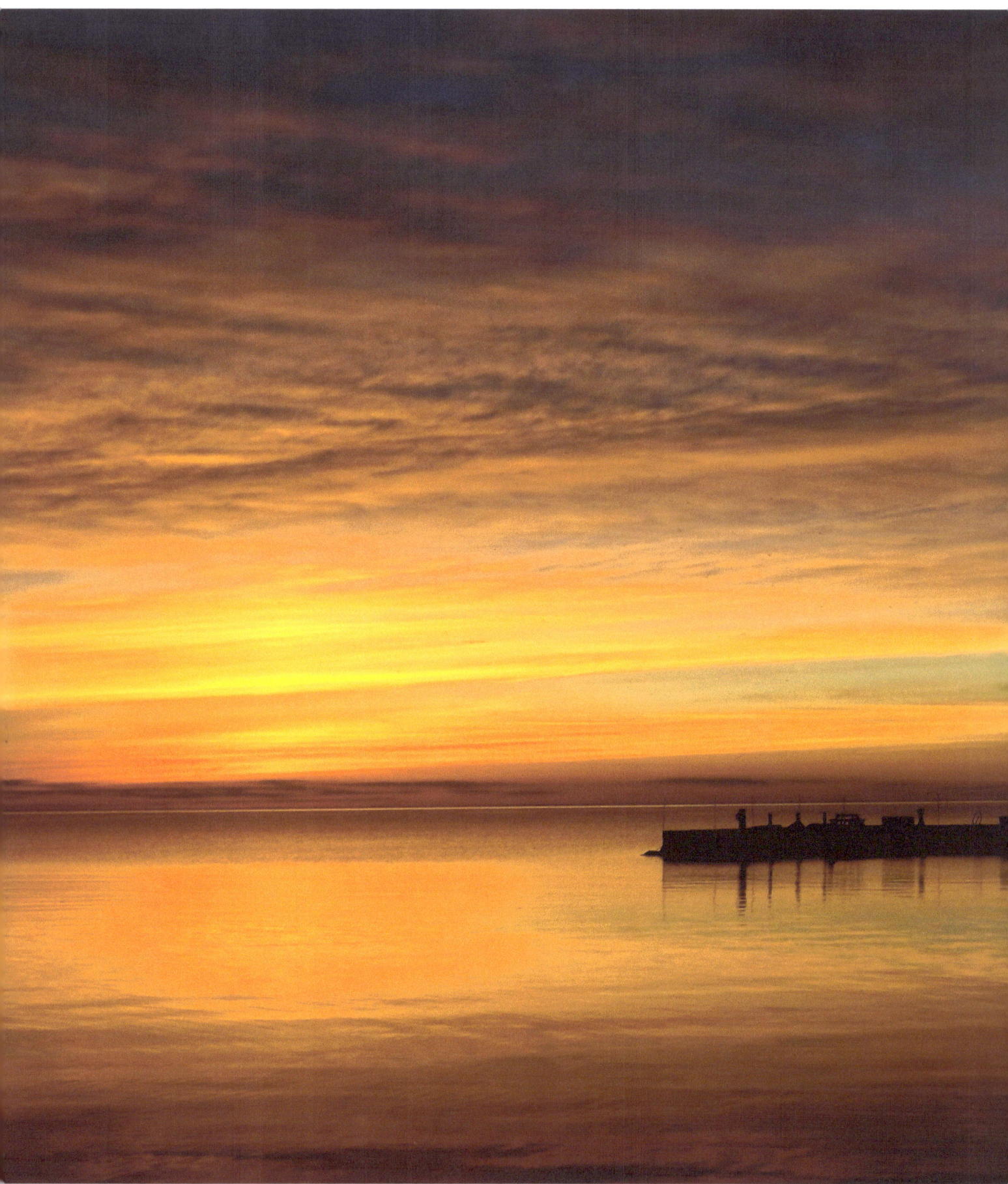

18—

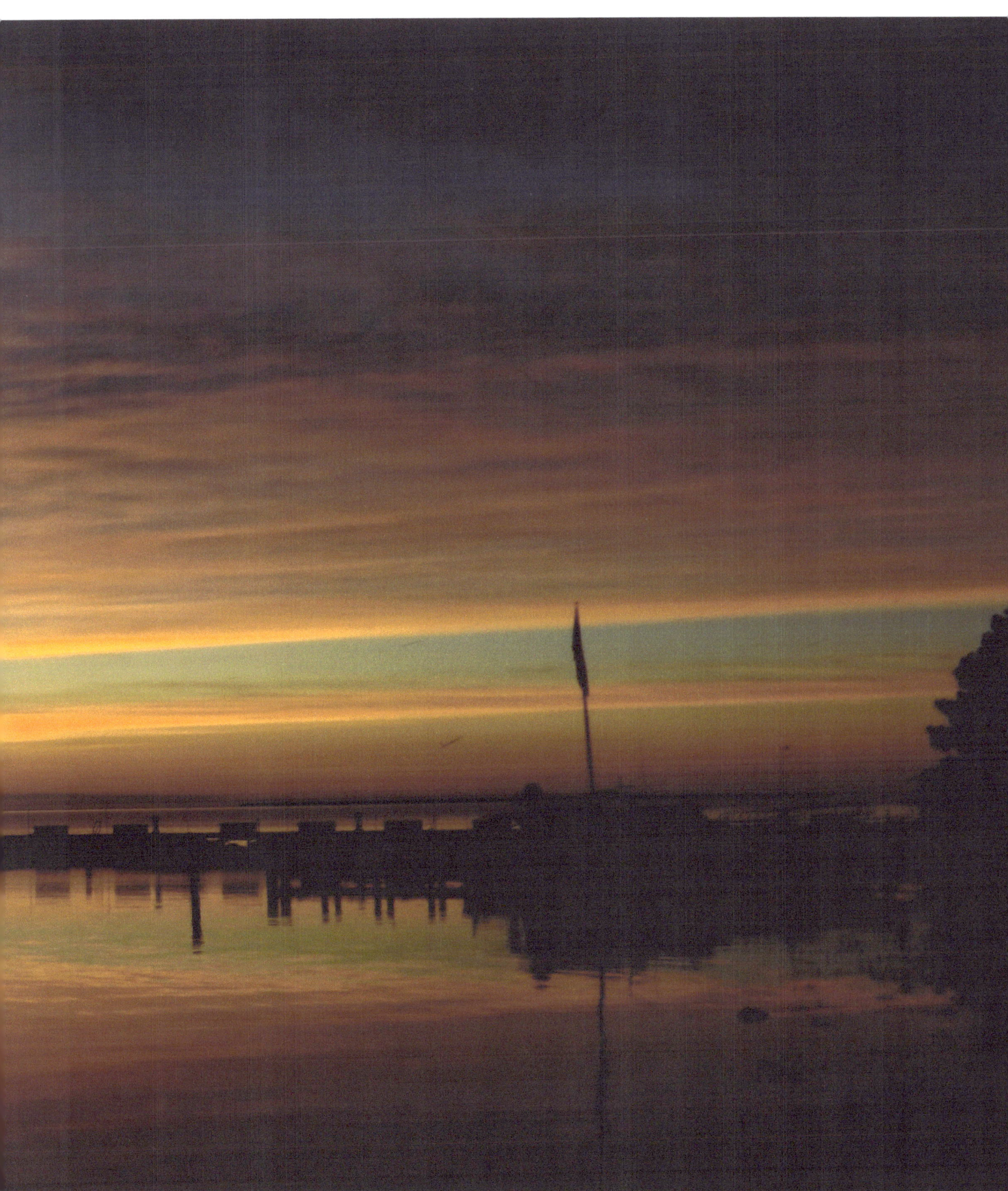

Dock Sunset at Egg Harbor Wisconsin v1

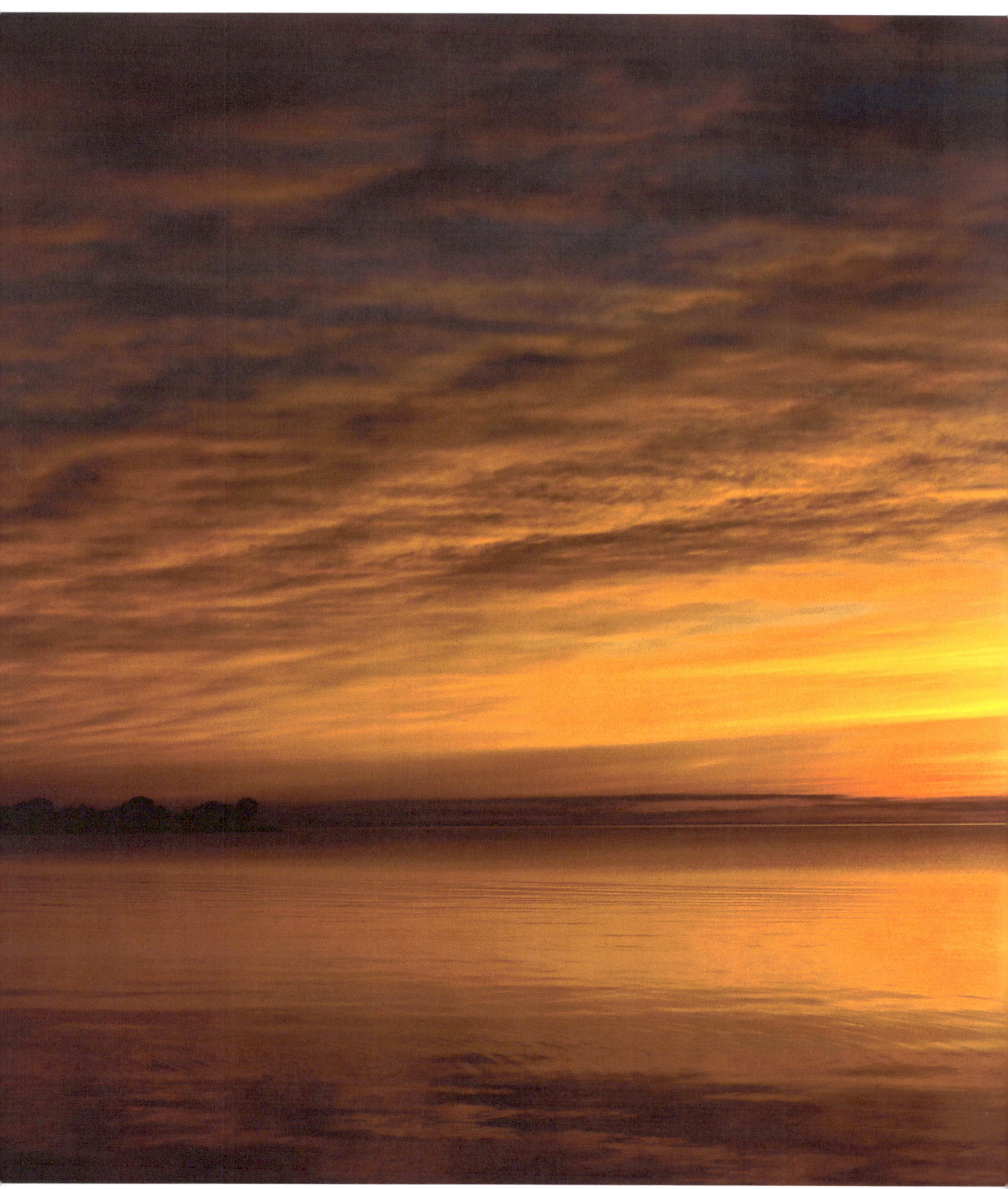

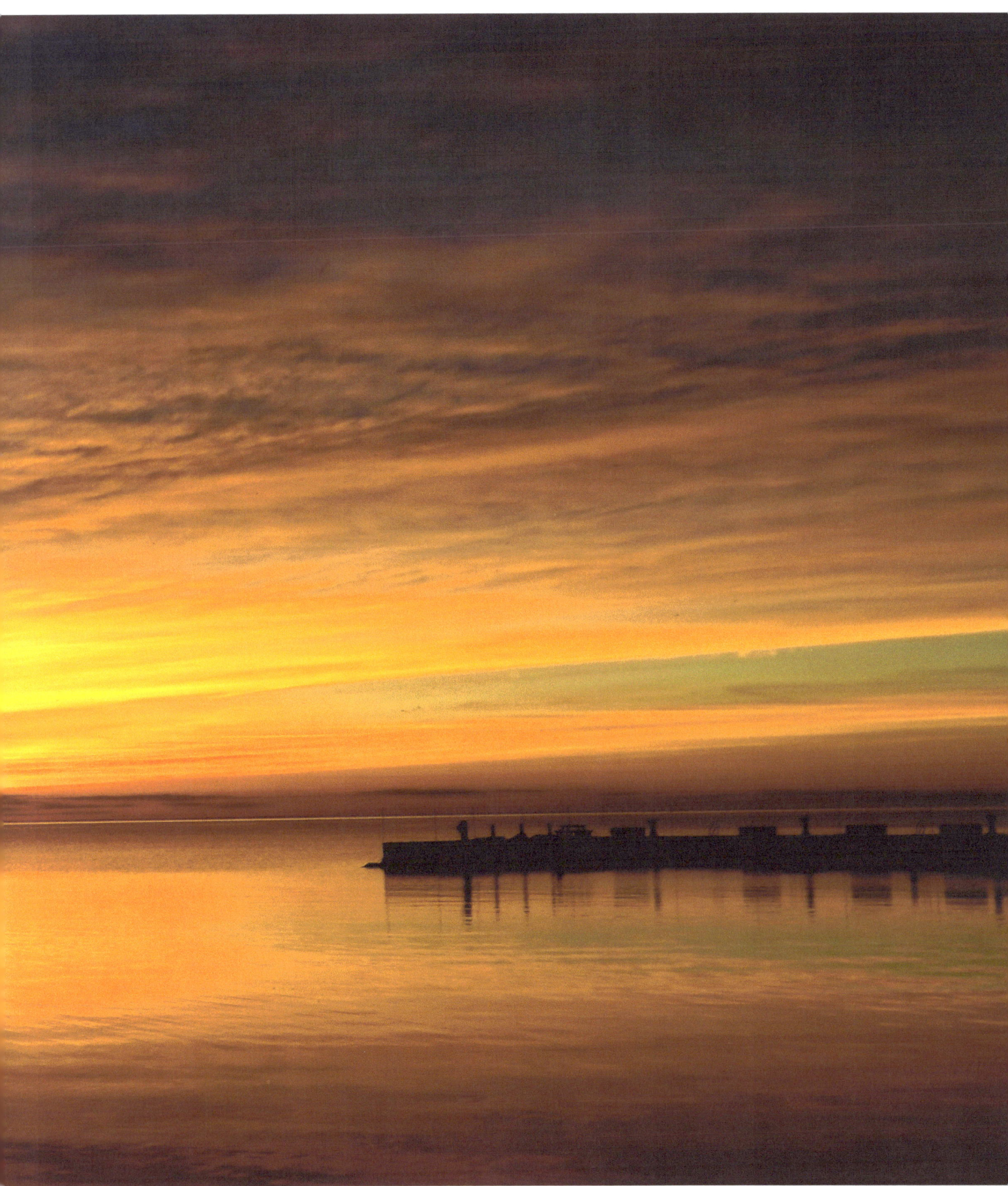

Dock Sunset at Egg Harbor Wisconsin v2

Egg Harbor Marina at Sunset

The Egg Harbor Marina at dusk is shown above. At right, the granite boulders sparkle while the sun dips below the horizon. The following pages show the shoreline and harbor at dusk. The moon shines over the harbor on page 25.

22—

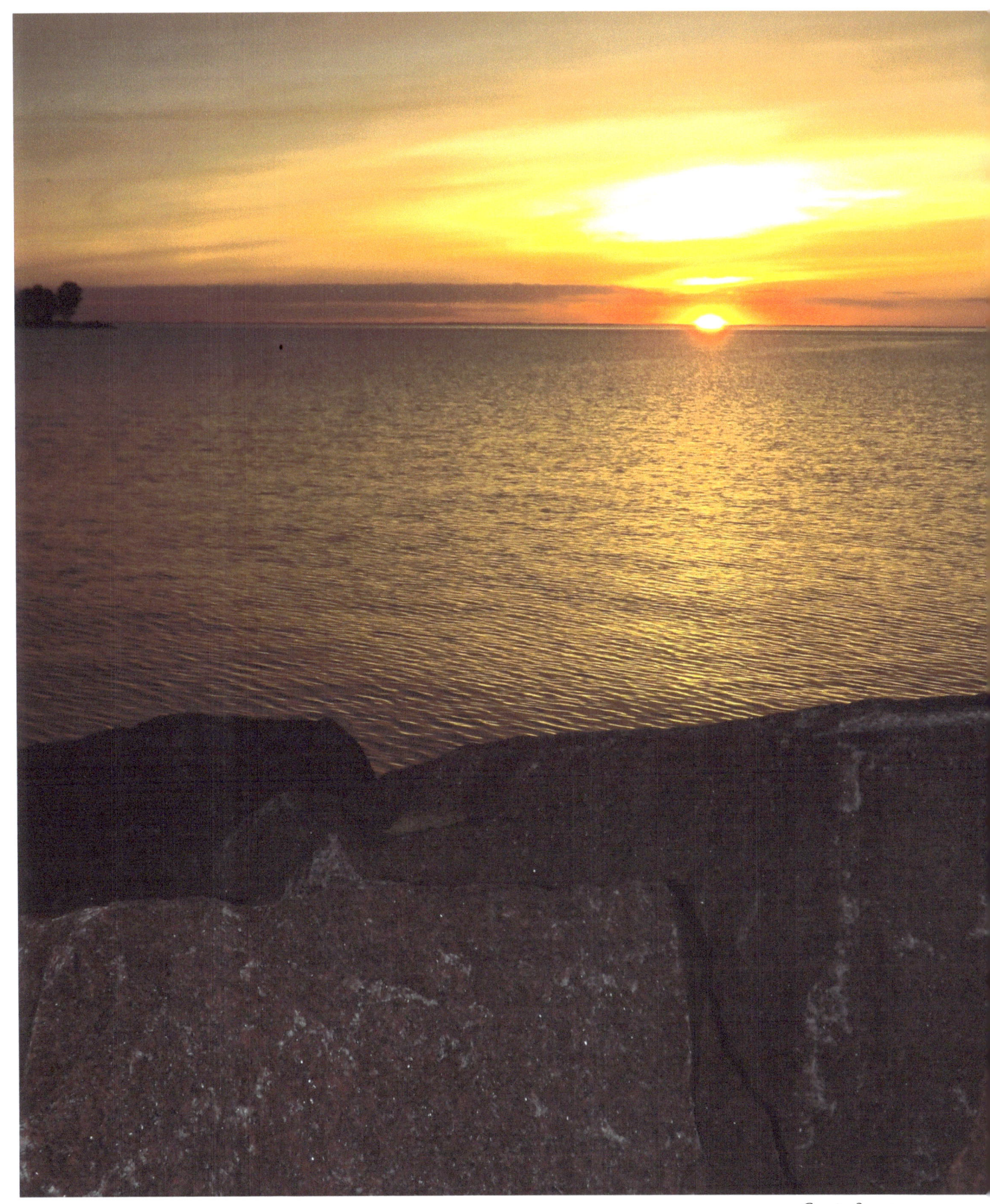

Granite Sunset

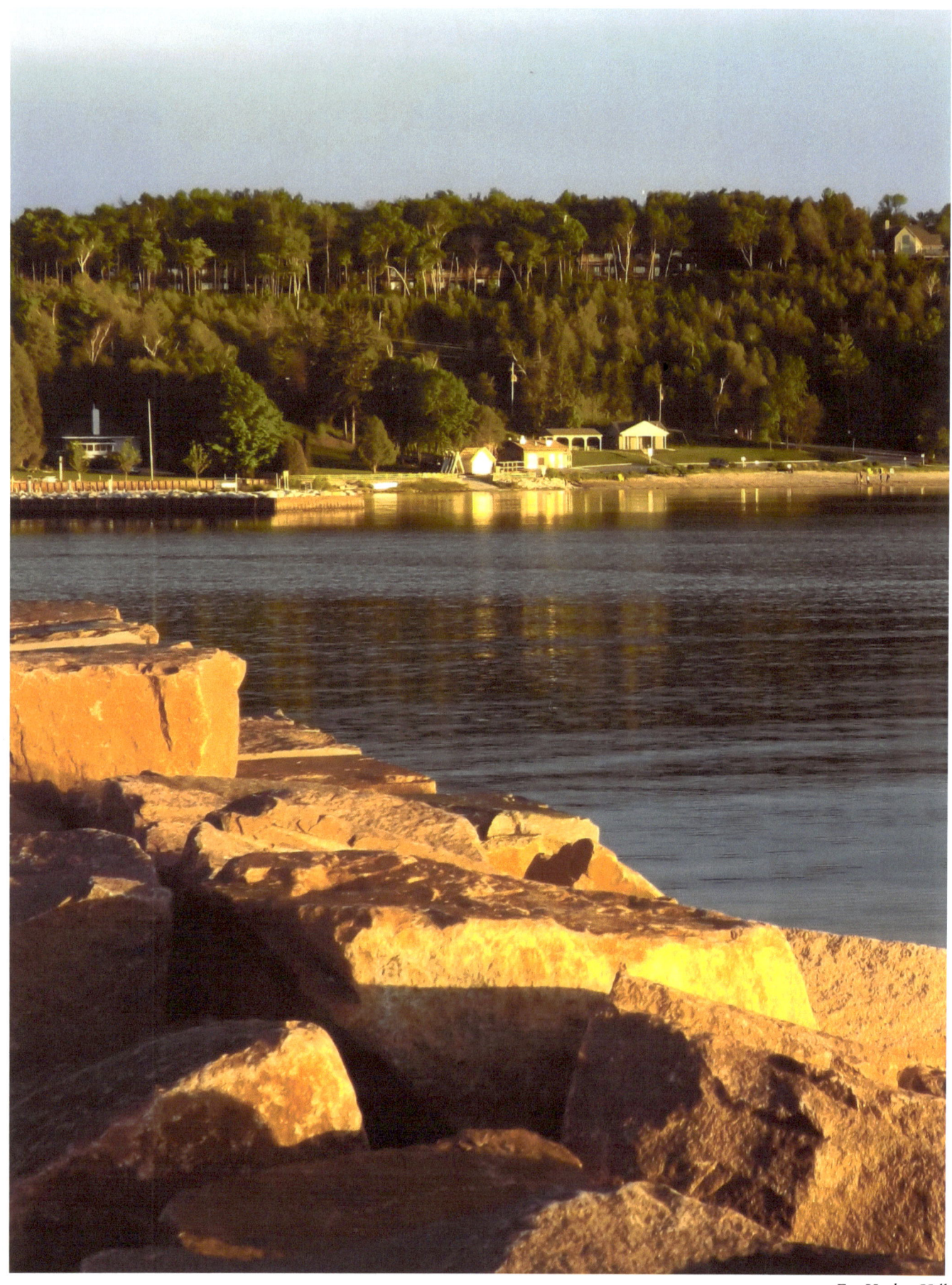

Egg Harbor Hill

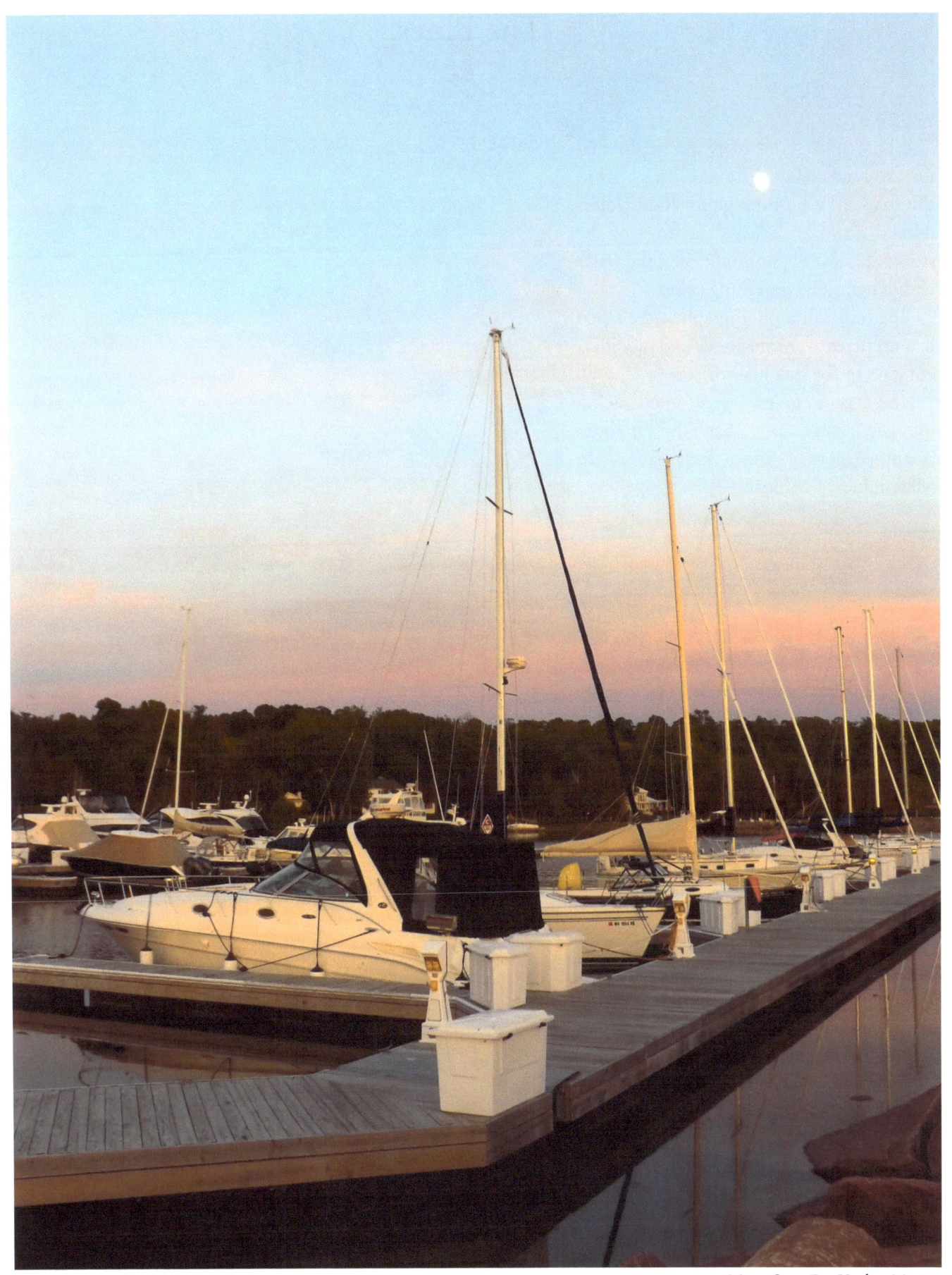

Moon Over Egg Harbor Marina

The Blues

The blues is a series of photographs that feature blue clouds. The one at right is in the shape of a hummingbird. Rain clouds draped down and passed in front of the sunset. Leftover light illuminated the water with a light blue refreshing color.

The remaining photographs were taken from different vantage points and on different days in the Egg Harbor area.

These photographs were taken facing the west across Green Bay. The far shore is approximately fifteen miles across to Menominee, Michigan.

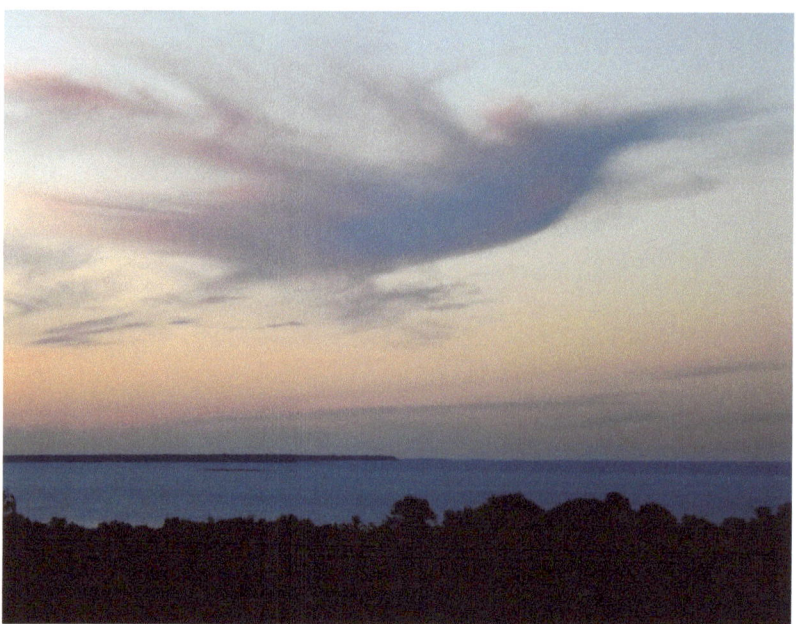

Hummingbird Cloud

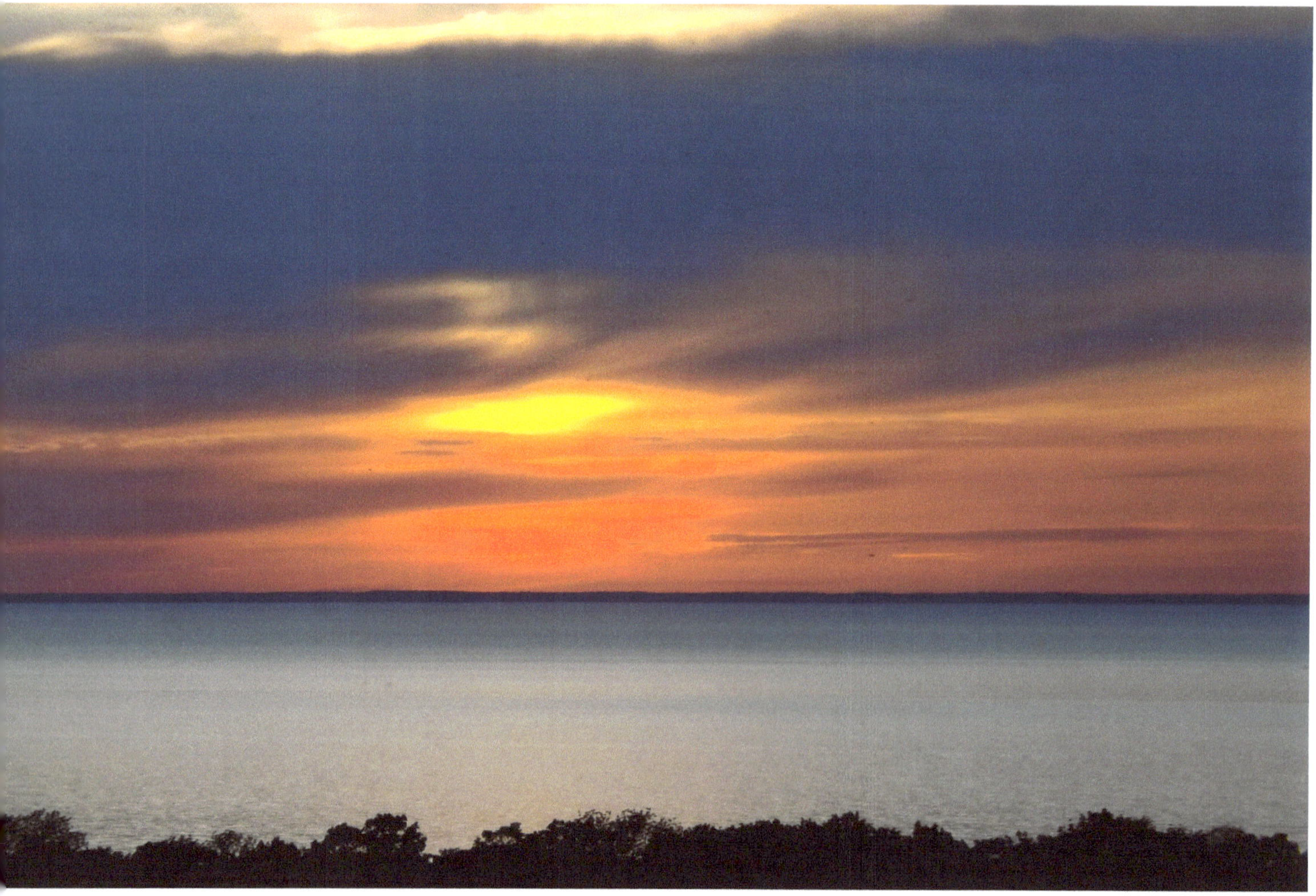

Rainy Sunset

Last Glow at Dusk

The Oranges and Reds

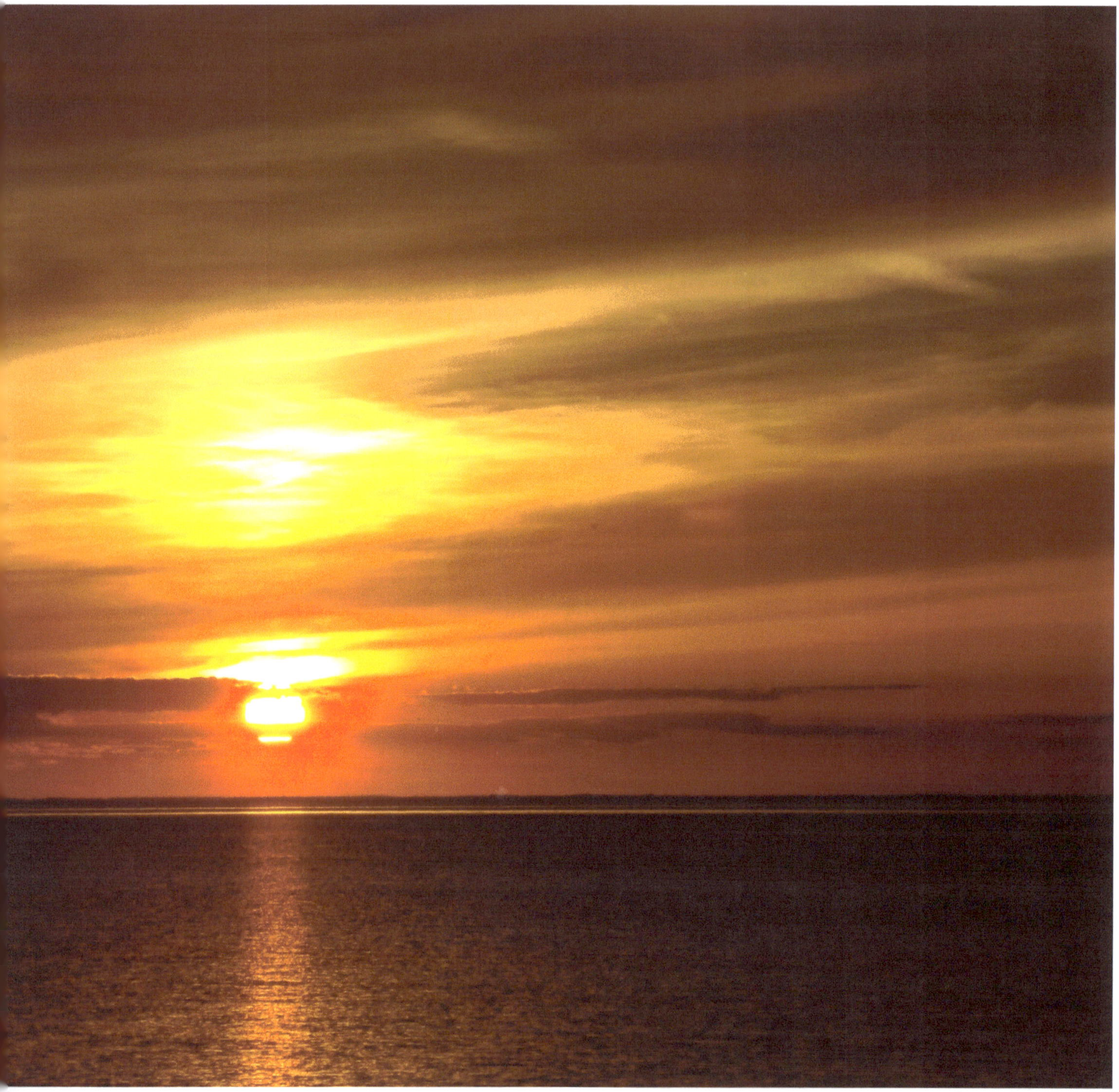

Red Sunset Number Four

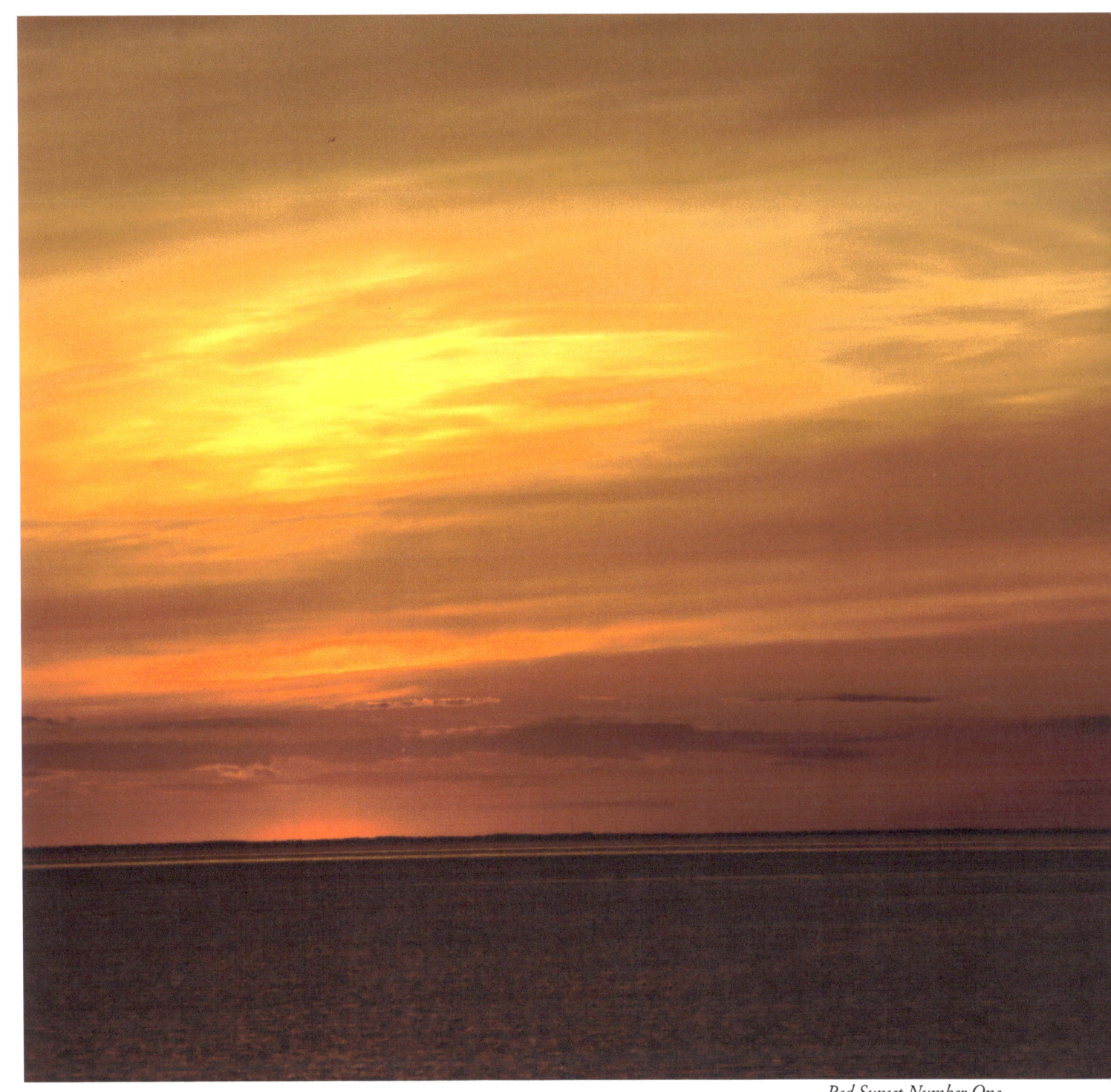

Red Sunset Number One

The following pages are a series of photographs with brilliant sunset oranges and reds from the Egg Harbor, Wisconsin area.

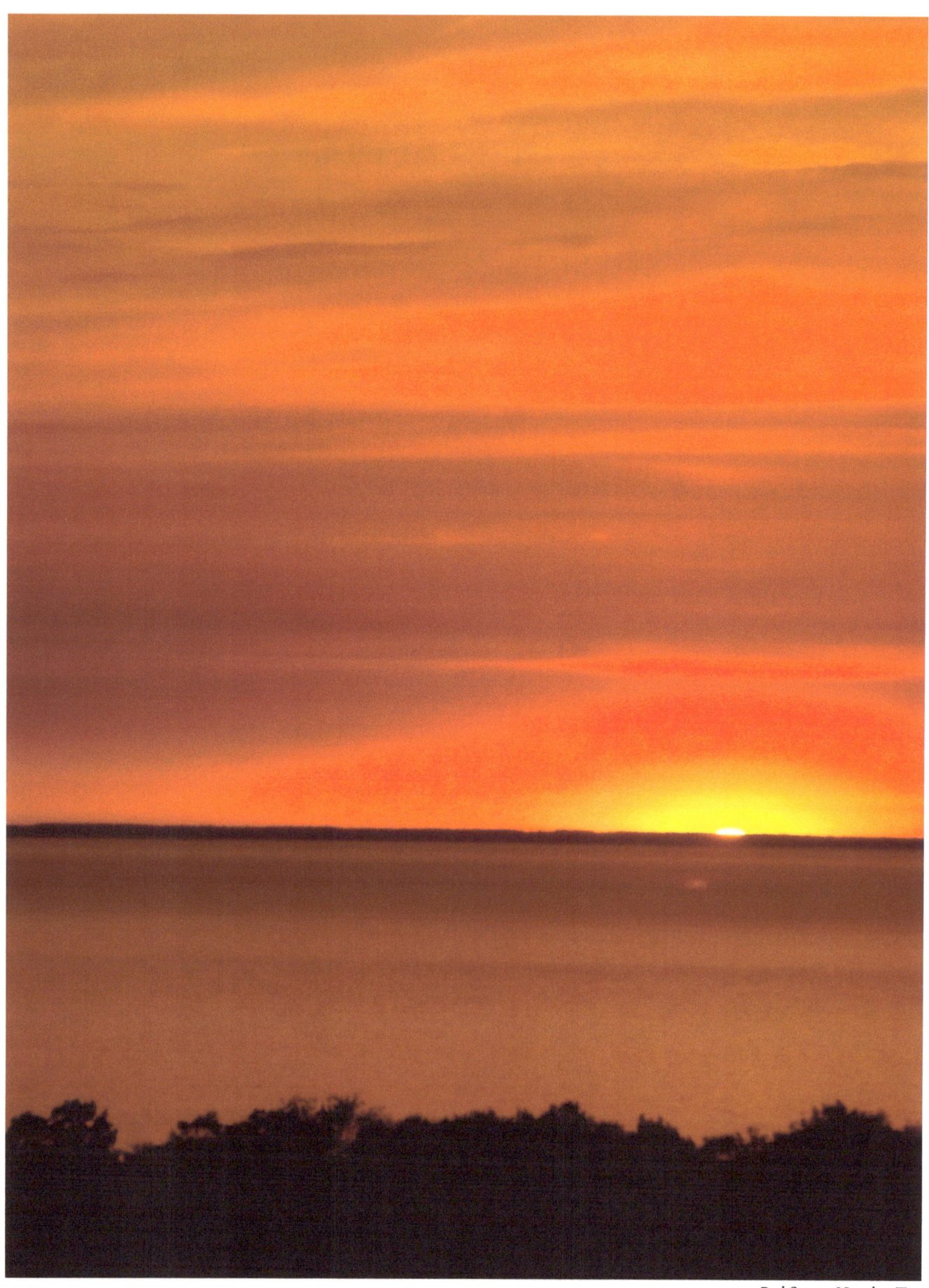

Red Sunset Number Two

Last Dash of Yellow Sunset

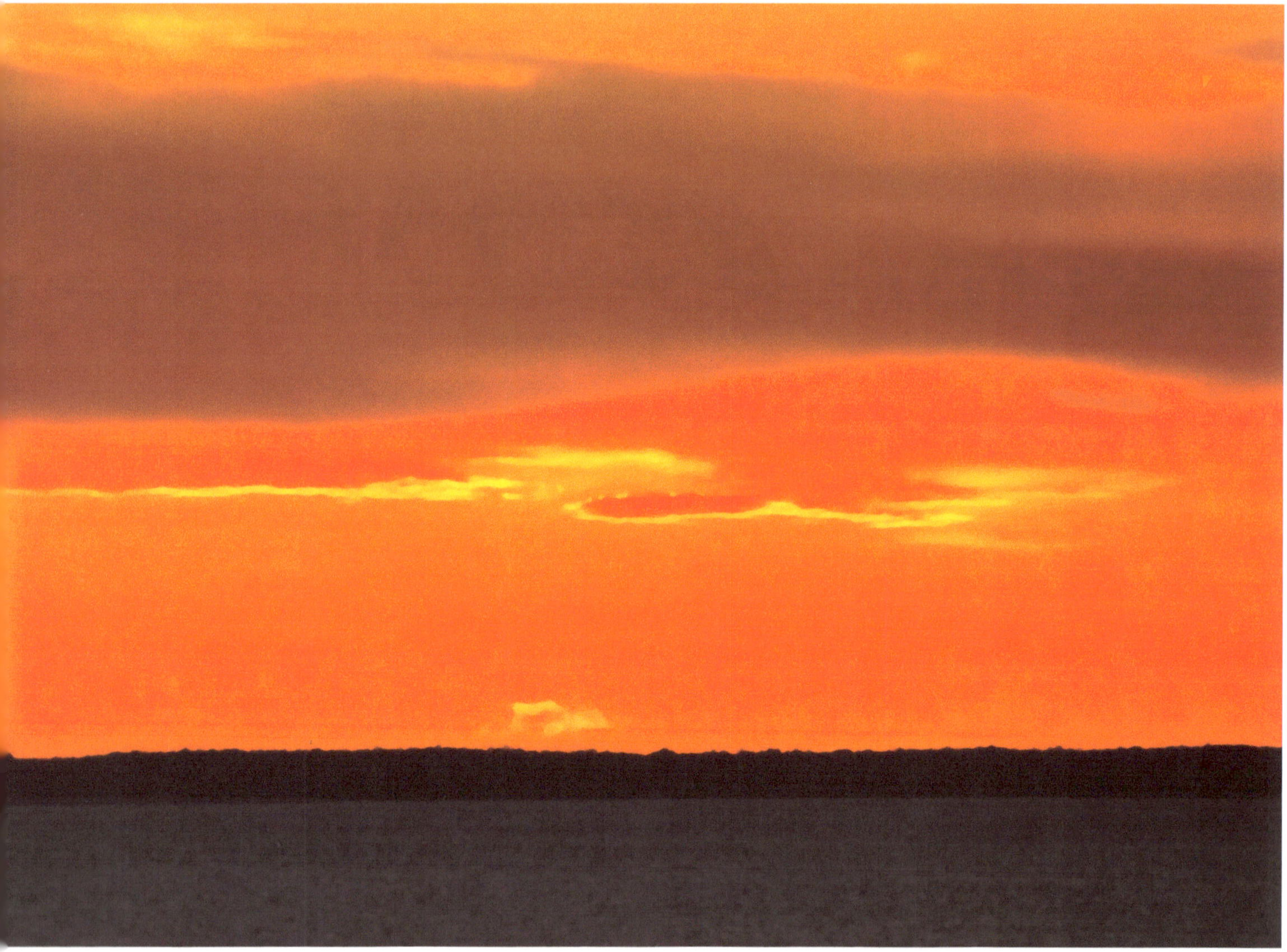

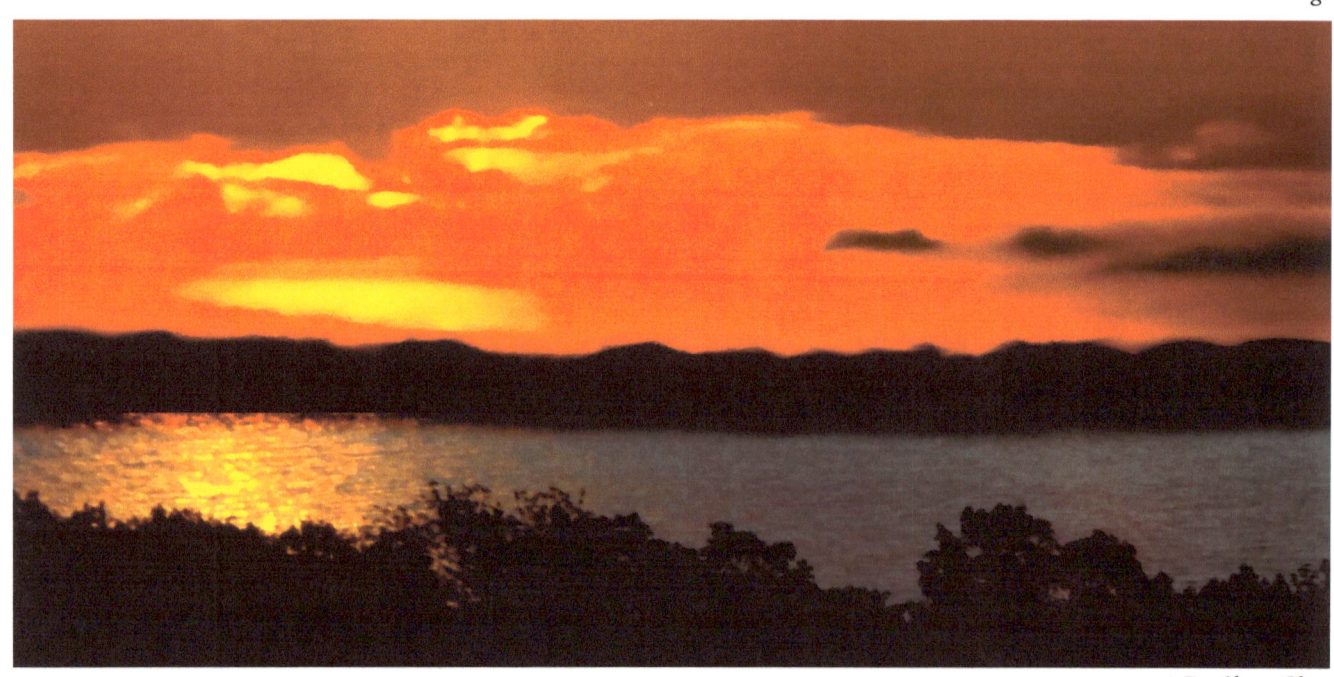

Sunset Orange

Far Shore Glow

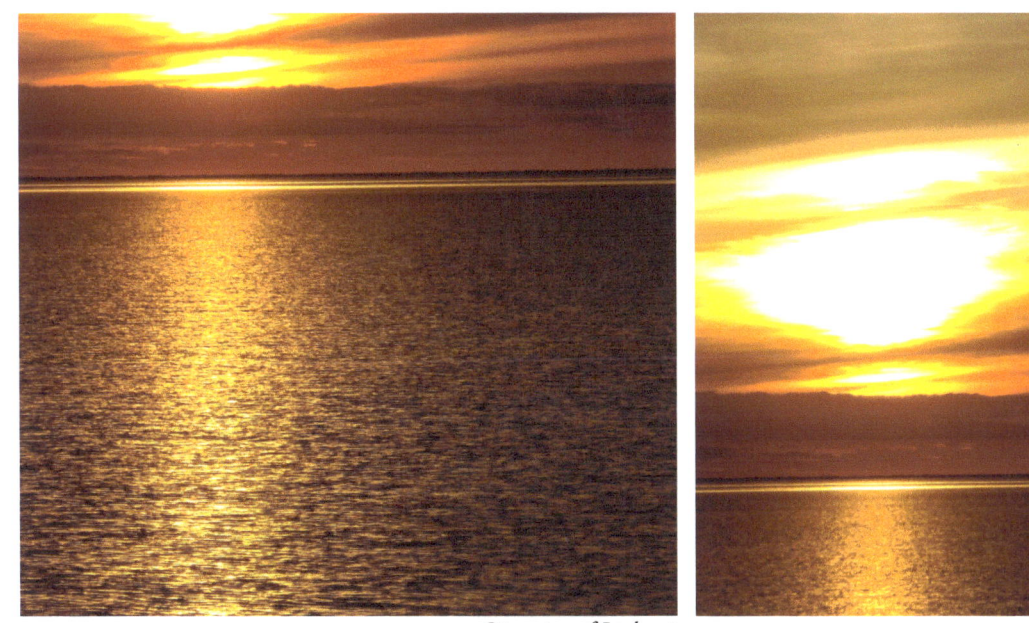

Pinstripe of Light v1

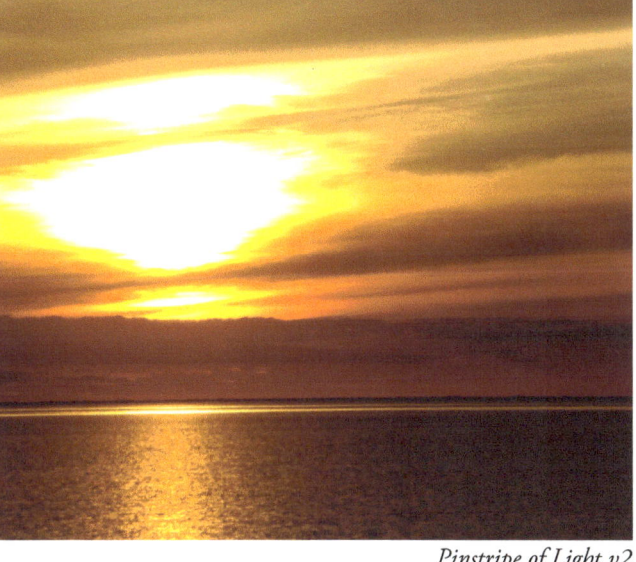

Pinstripe of Light v2

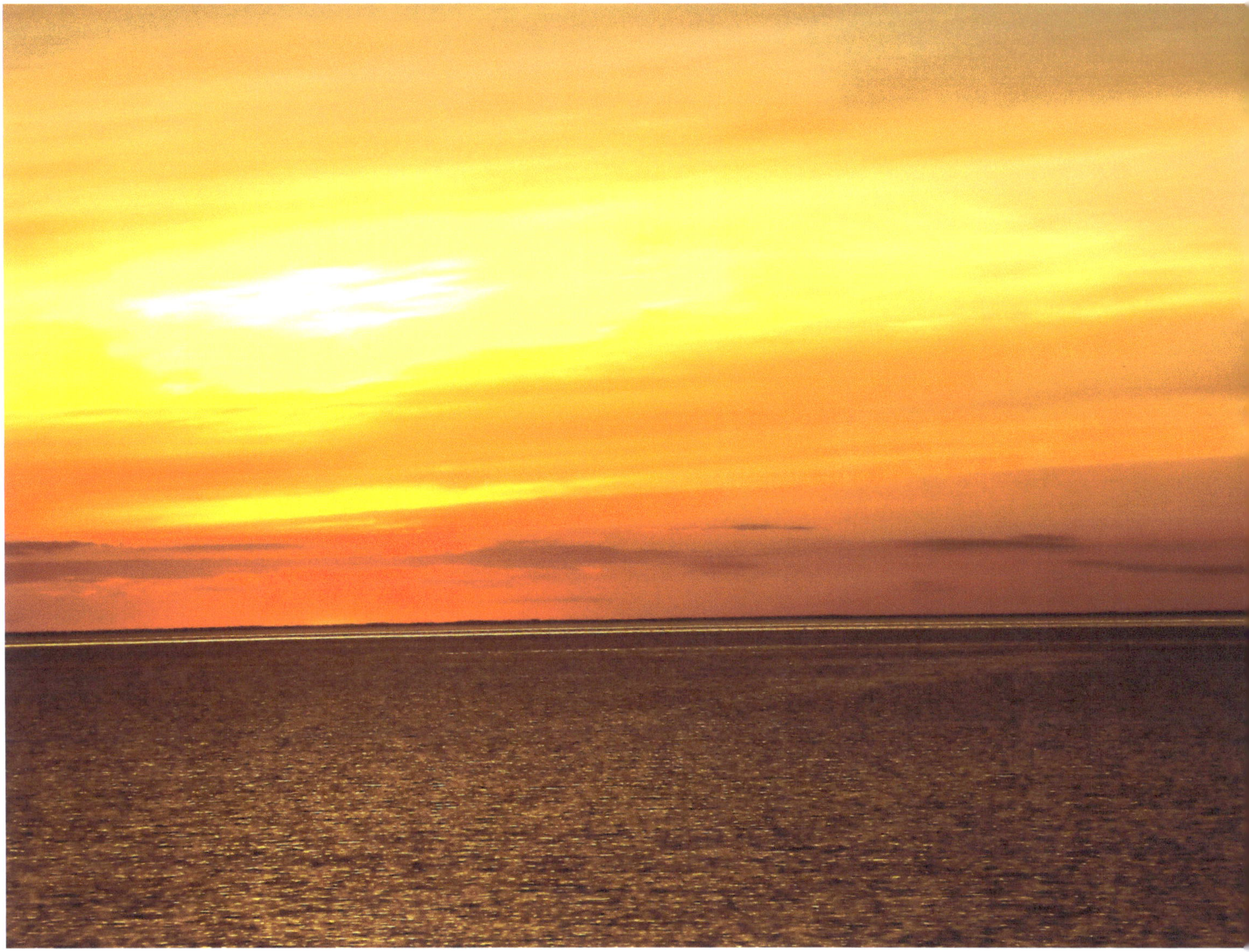

Pinstripe of Light v3

The Trees

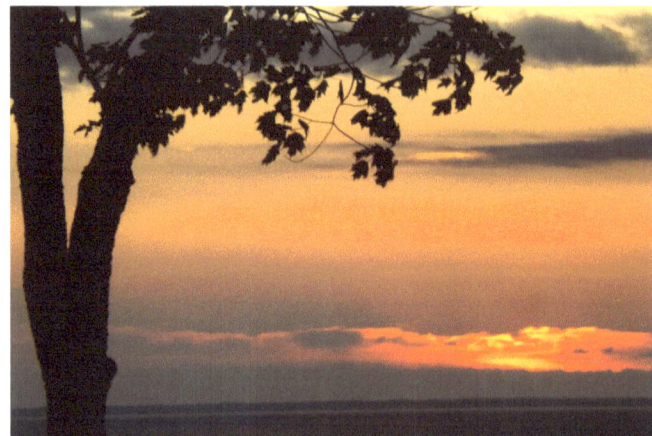

Last Glimmer of Sunset

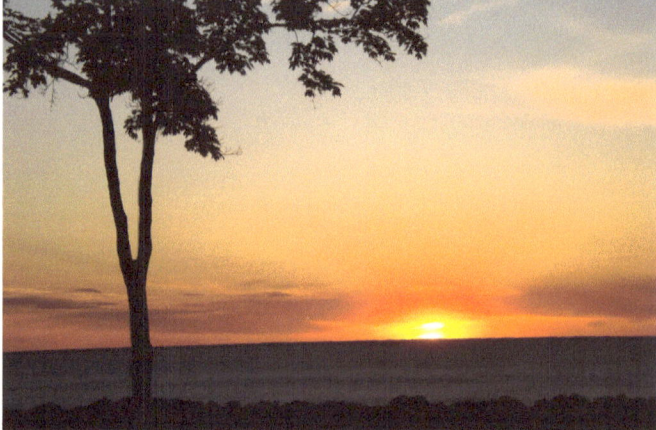

Calm Sunset

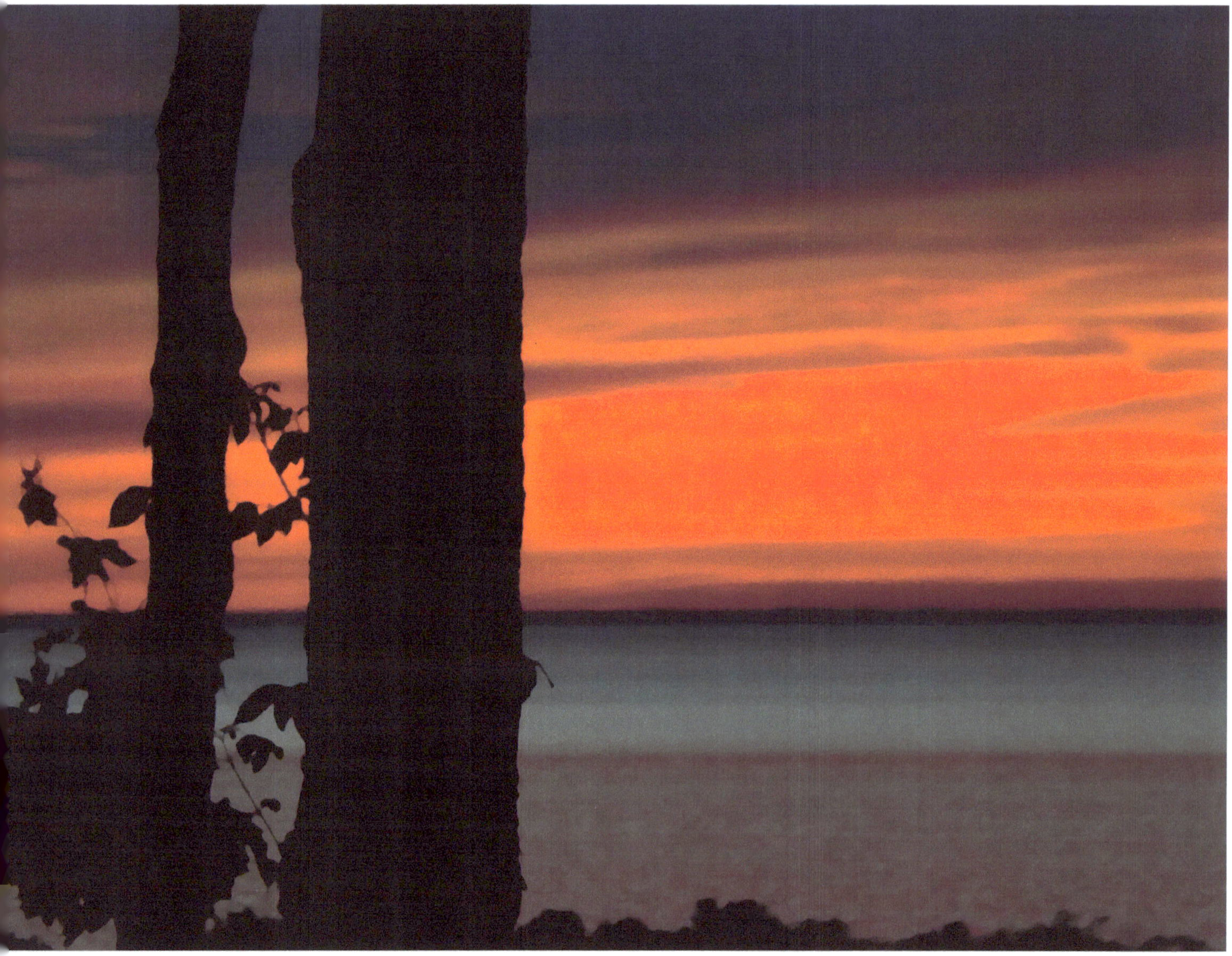

Cool Blues Sunset, Oil Painting Effect

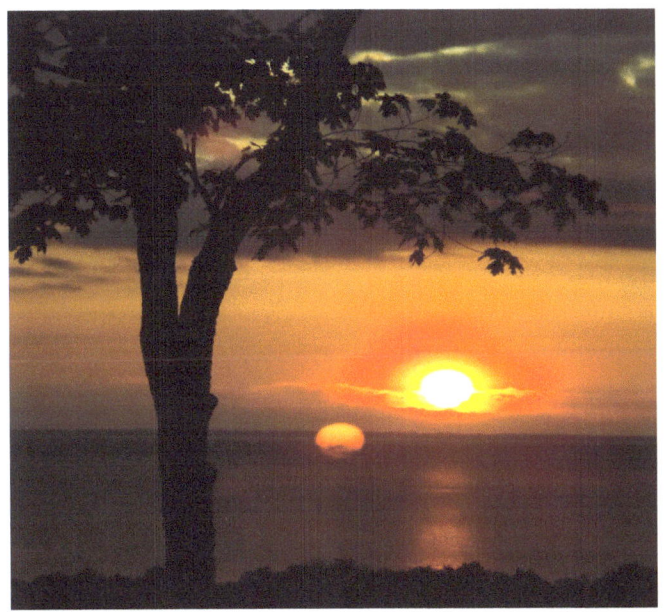

Double Sun Sunset

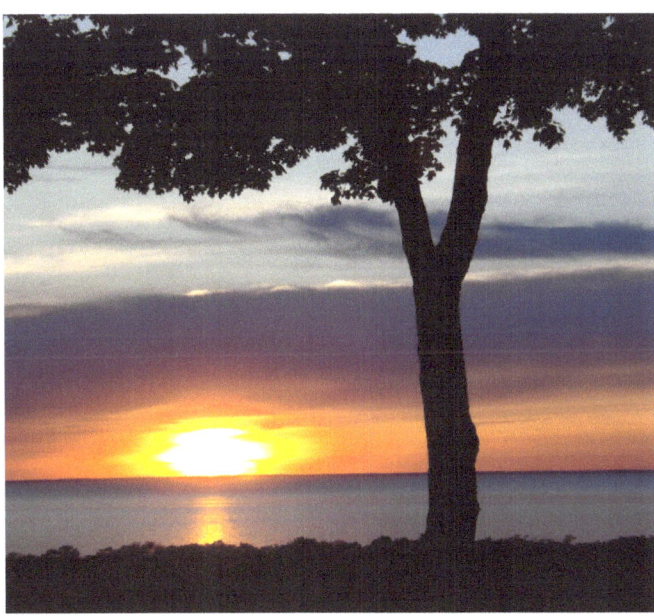

Silhouette Sunset Number One

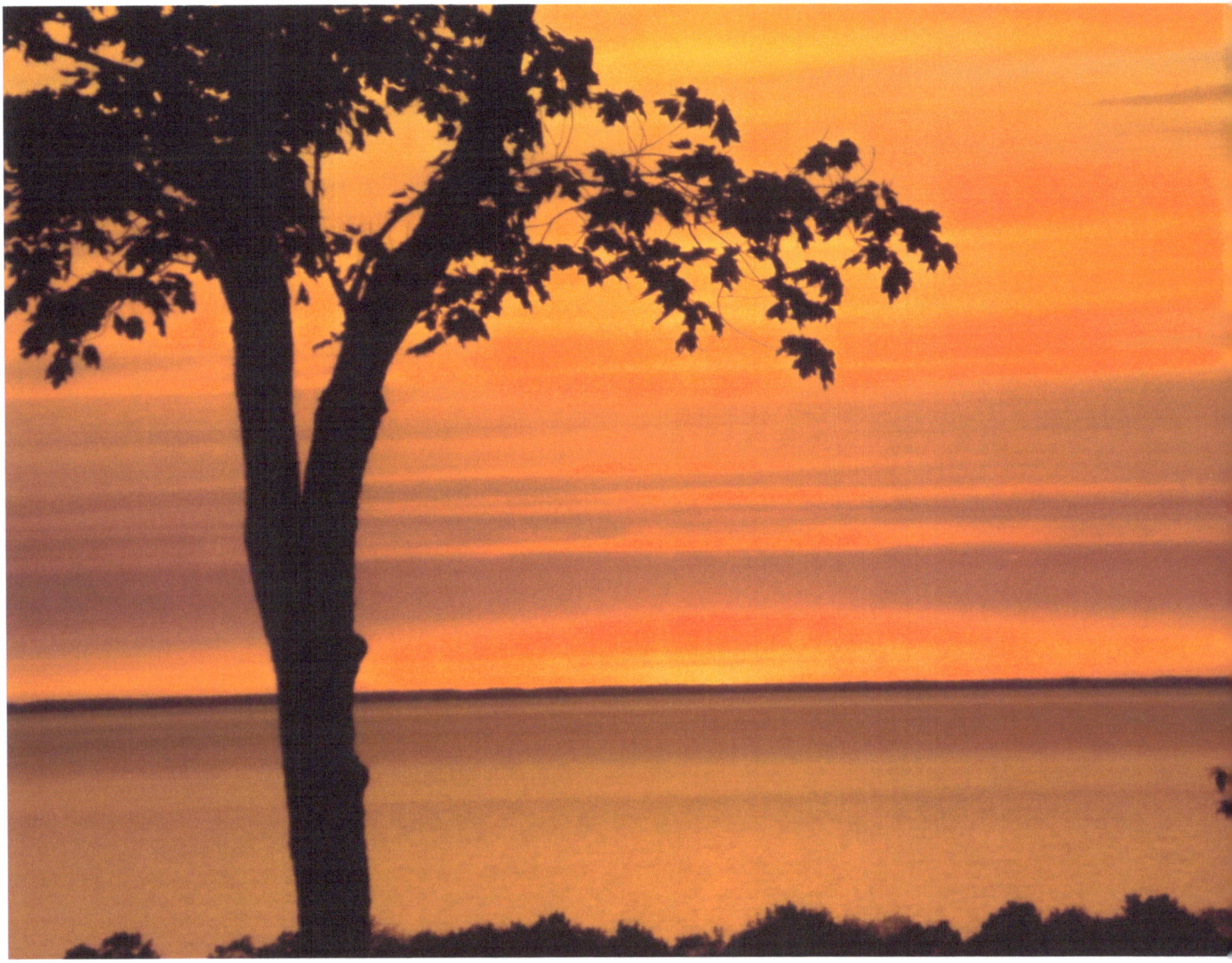

Orange Sunset

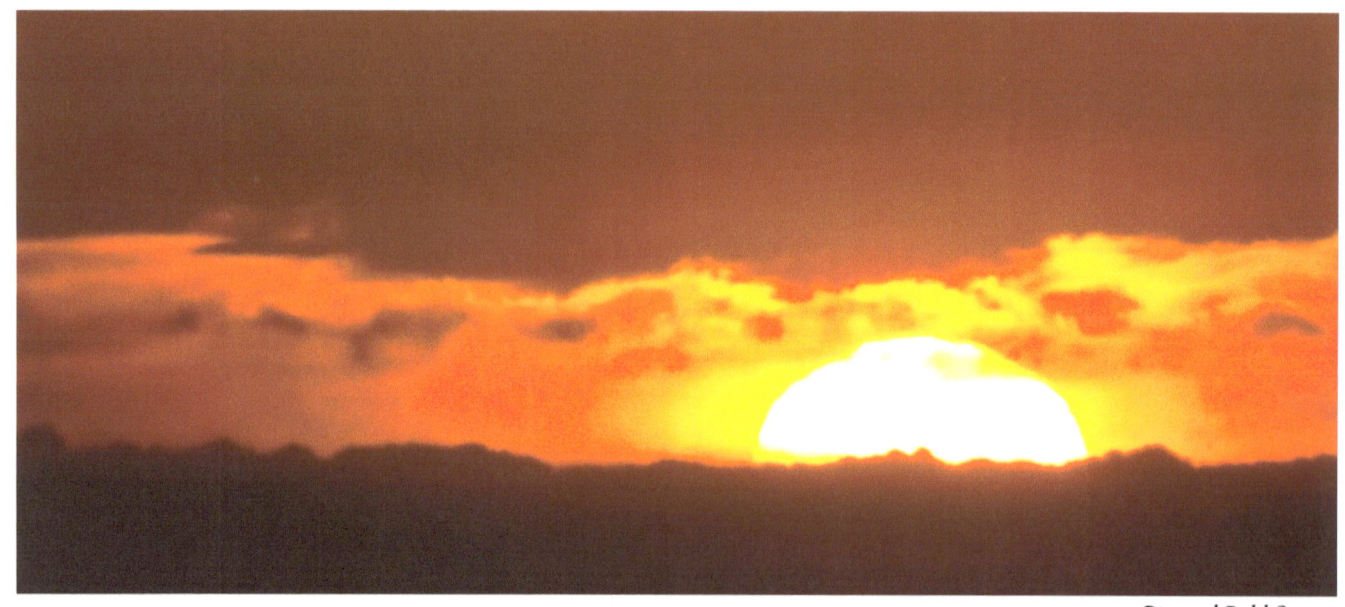

Big and Bold Sunset

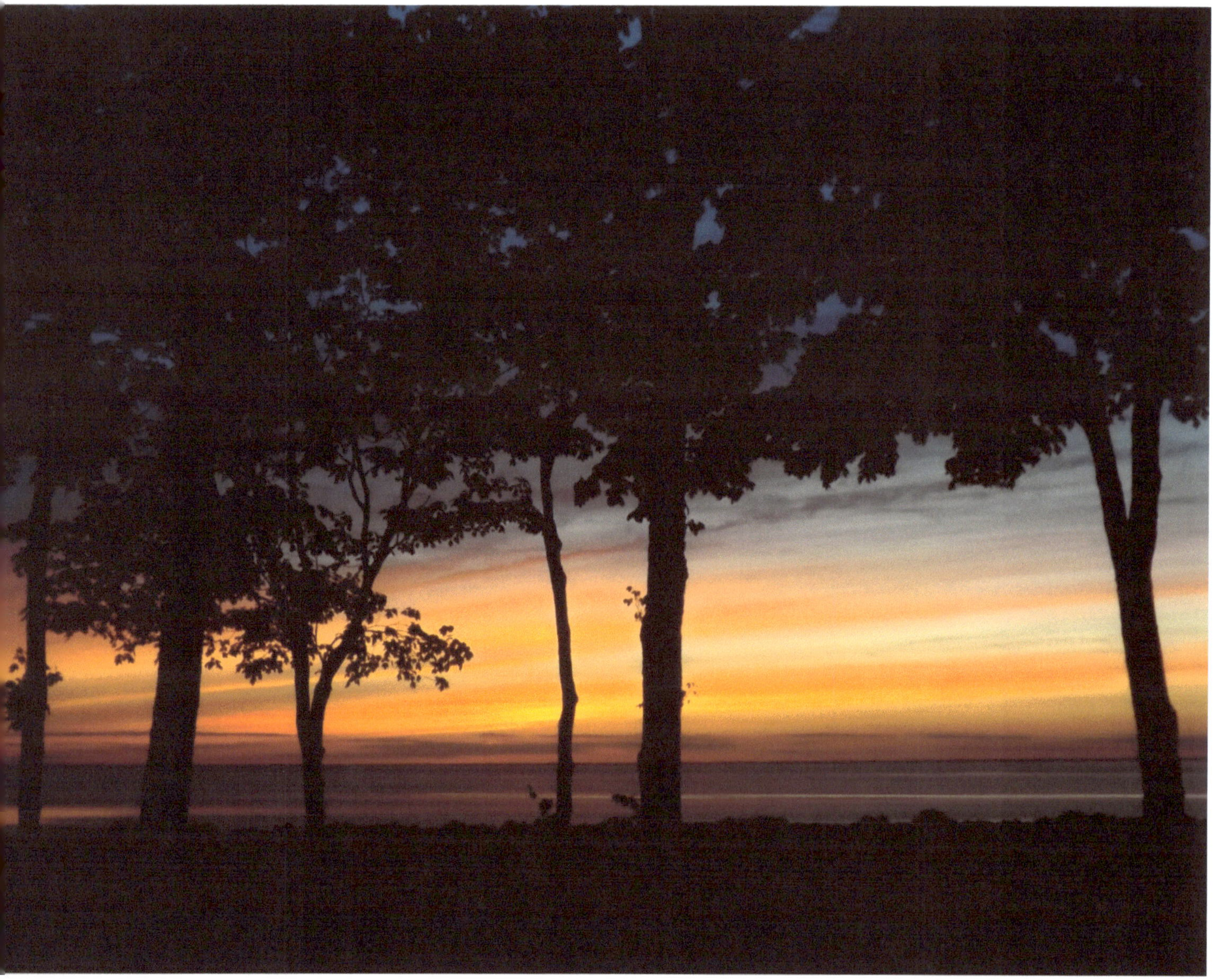

Striped Pastel Sunset Number One

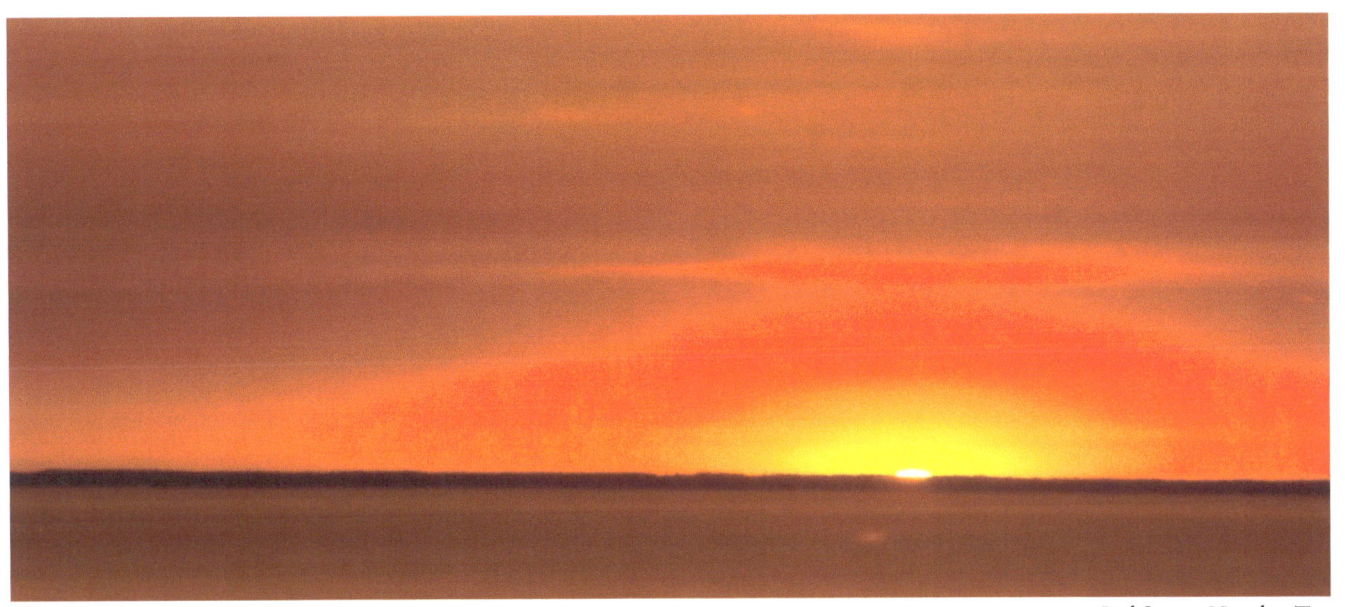

Red Sunset Number Two

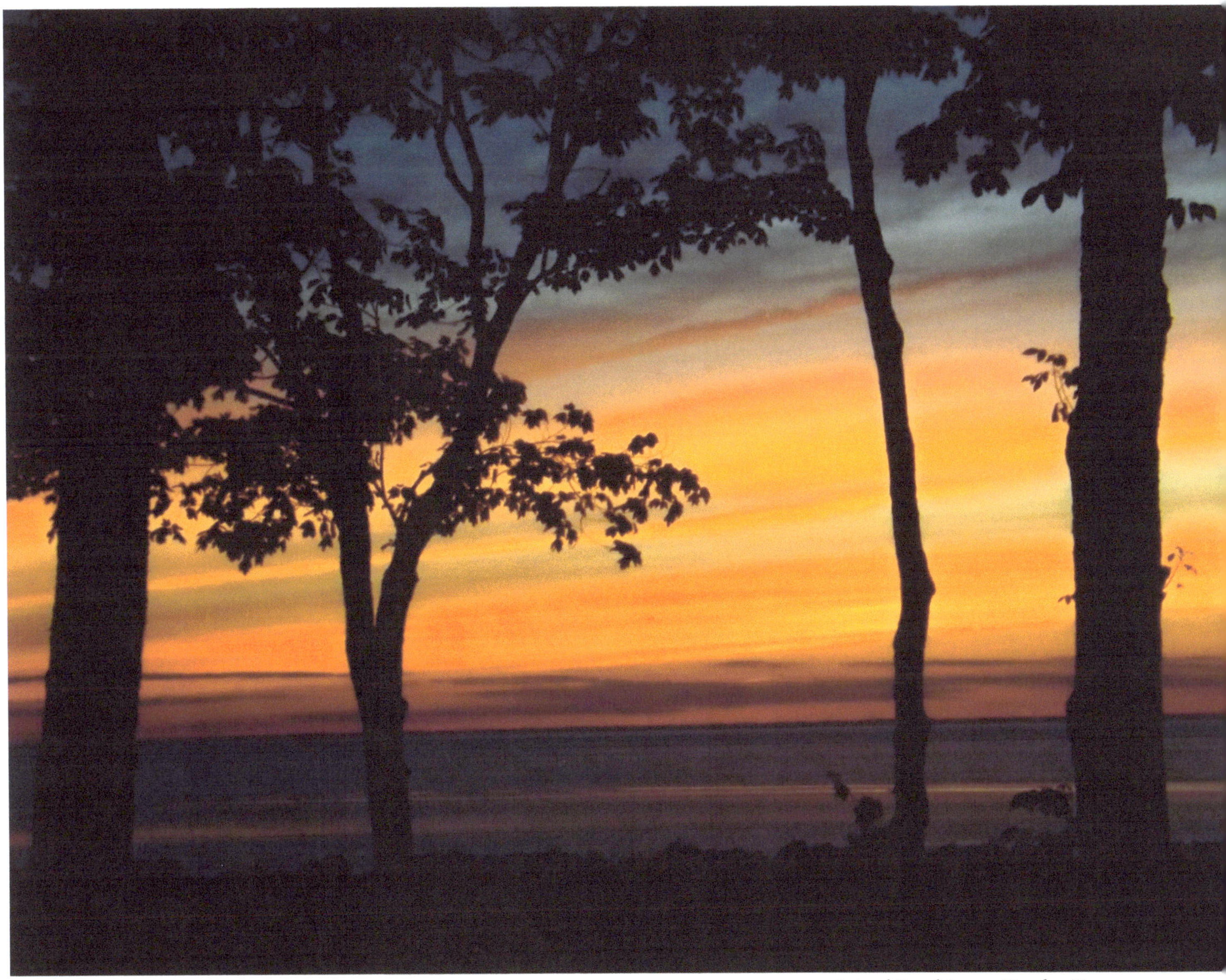

Striped Pastel Sunset Number Two

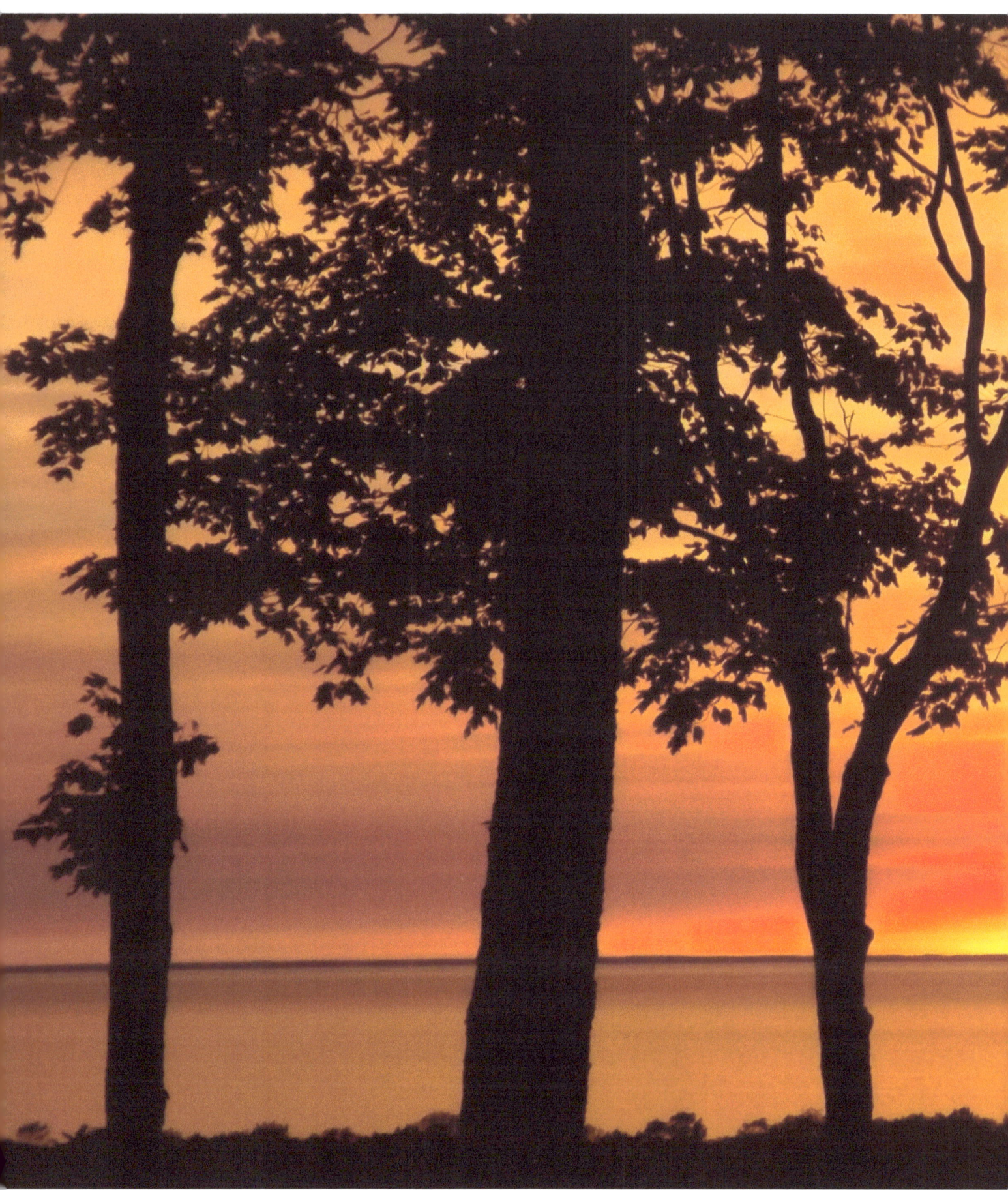

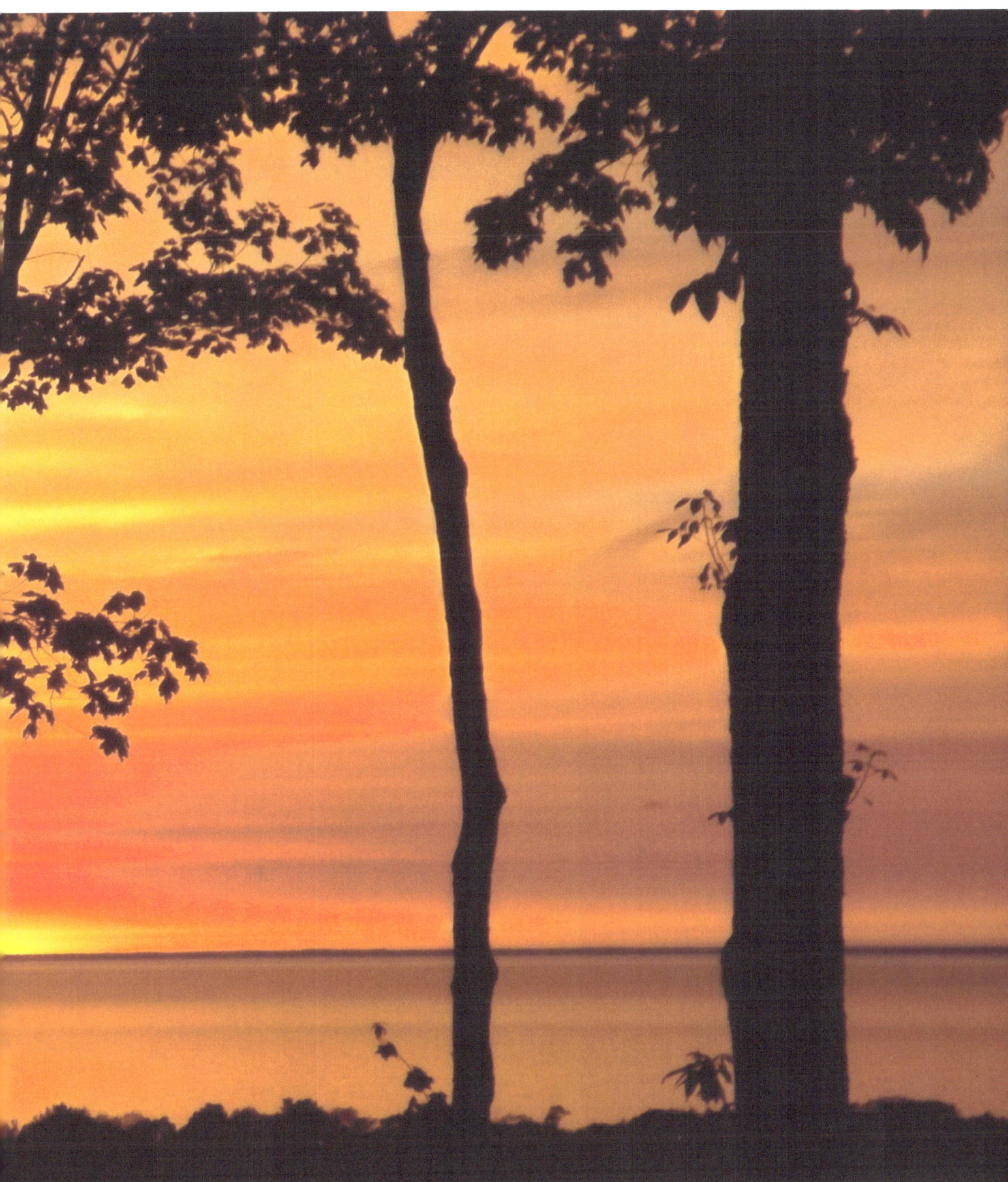

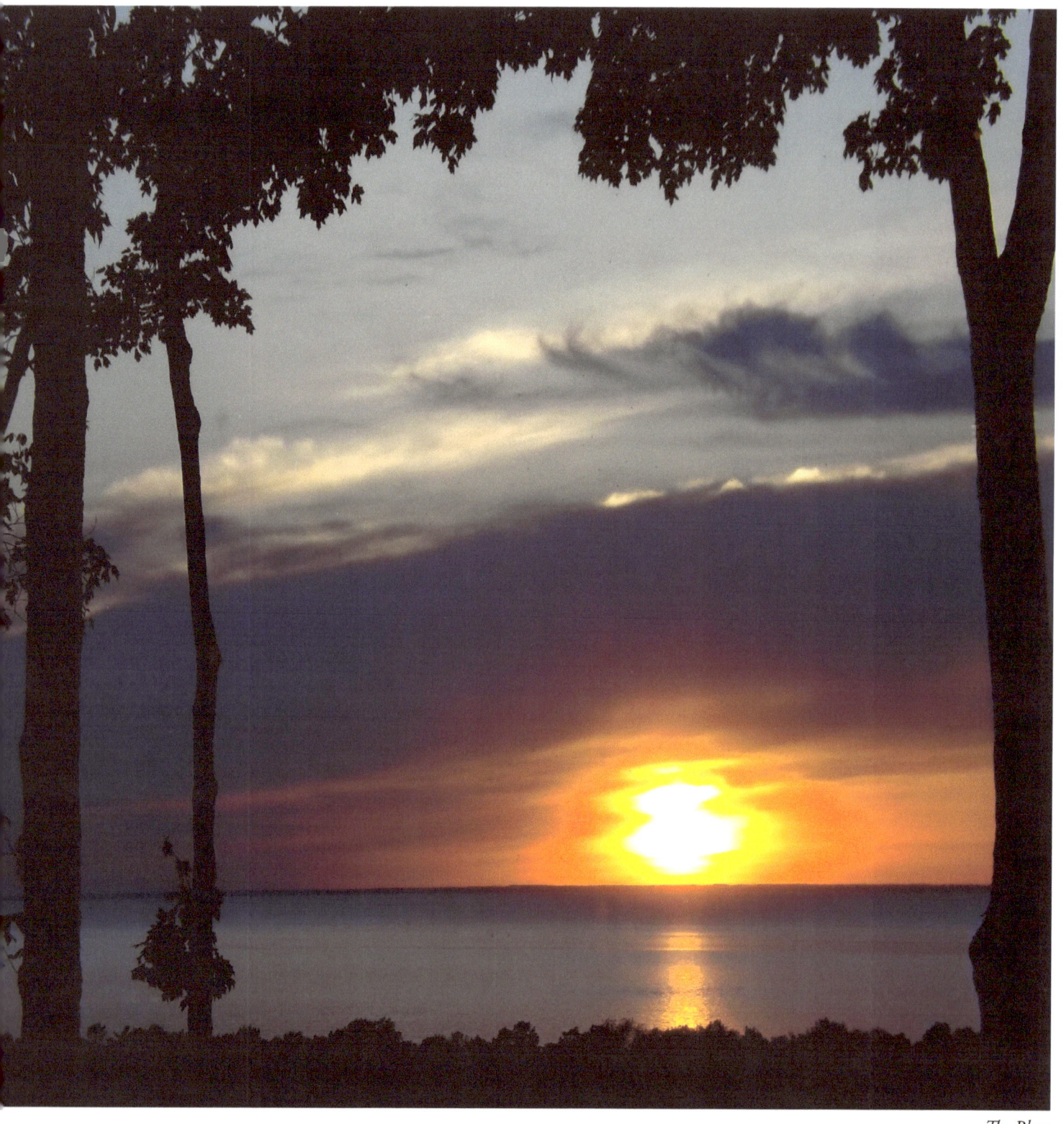

The Blues

Trees silhouetted against the sunset adds dramatic effect. The photo on the right, displays multiple suns from the reflection against a glass window.

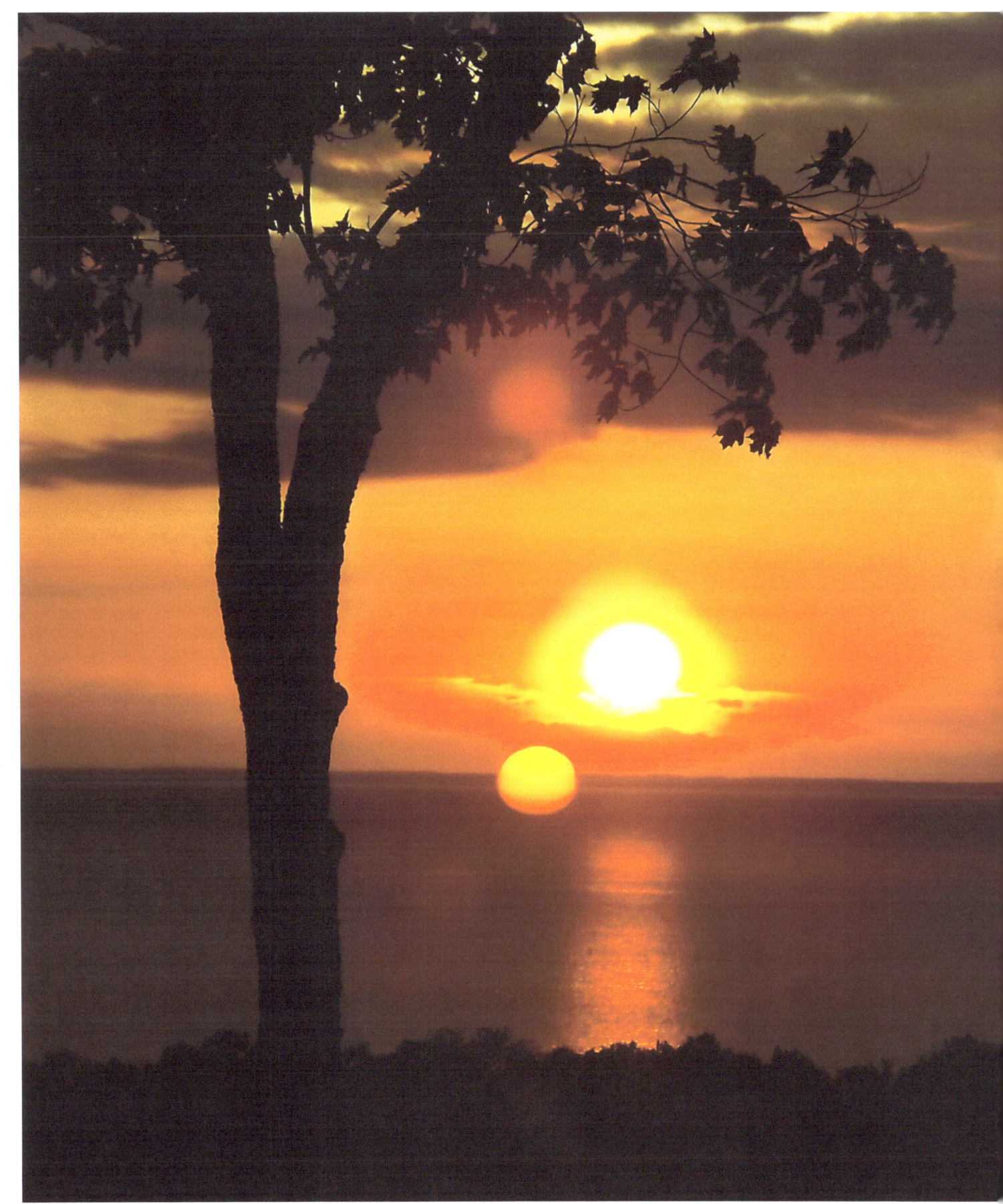

All My Suns

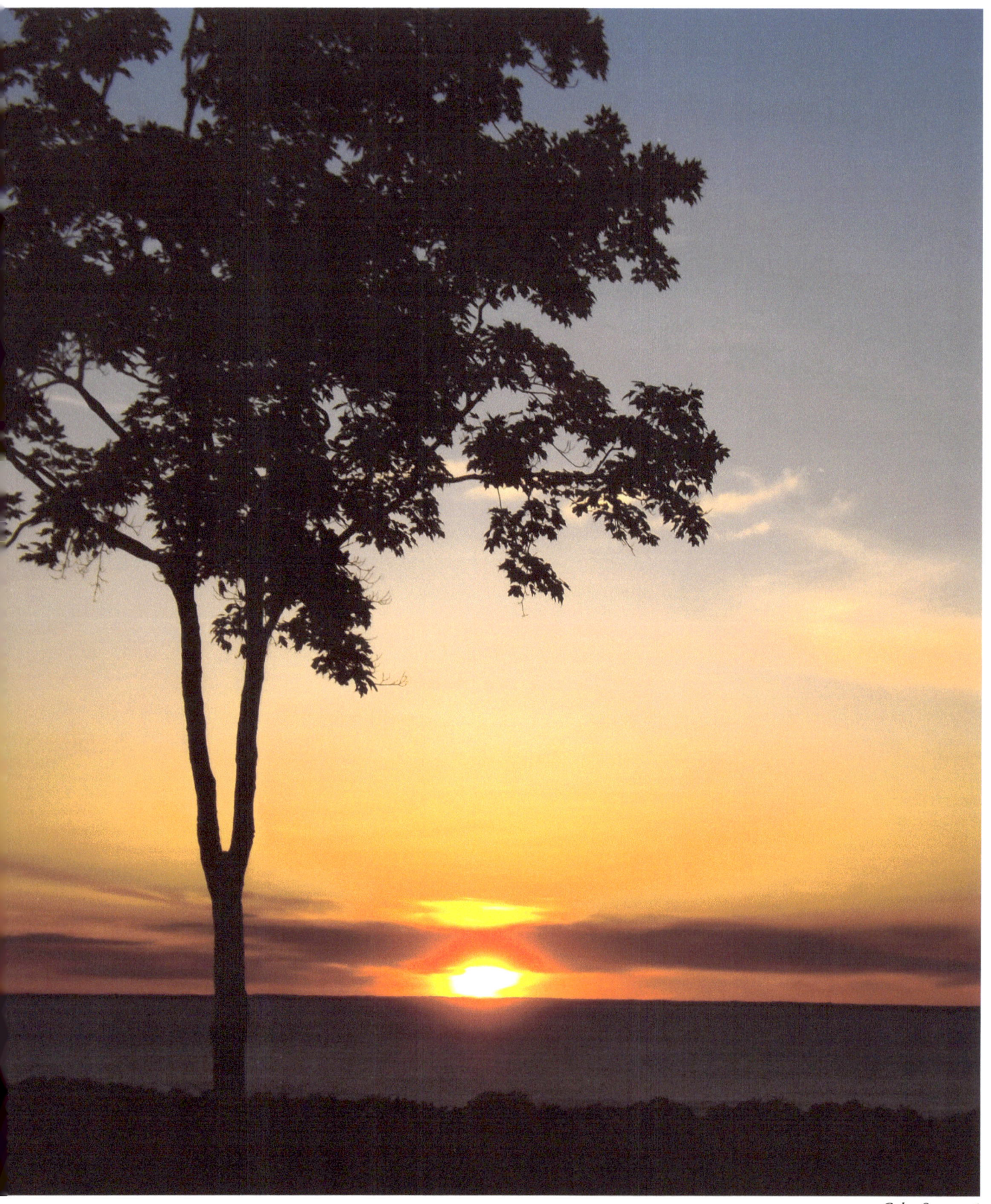

Calm Sunset v1

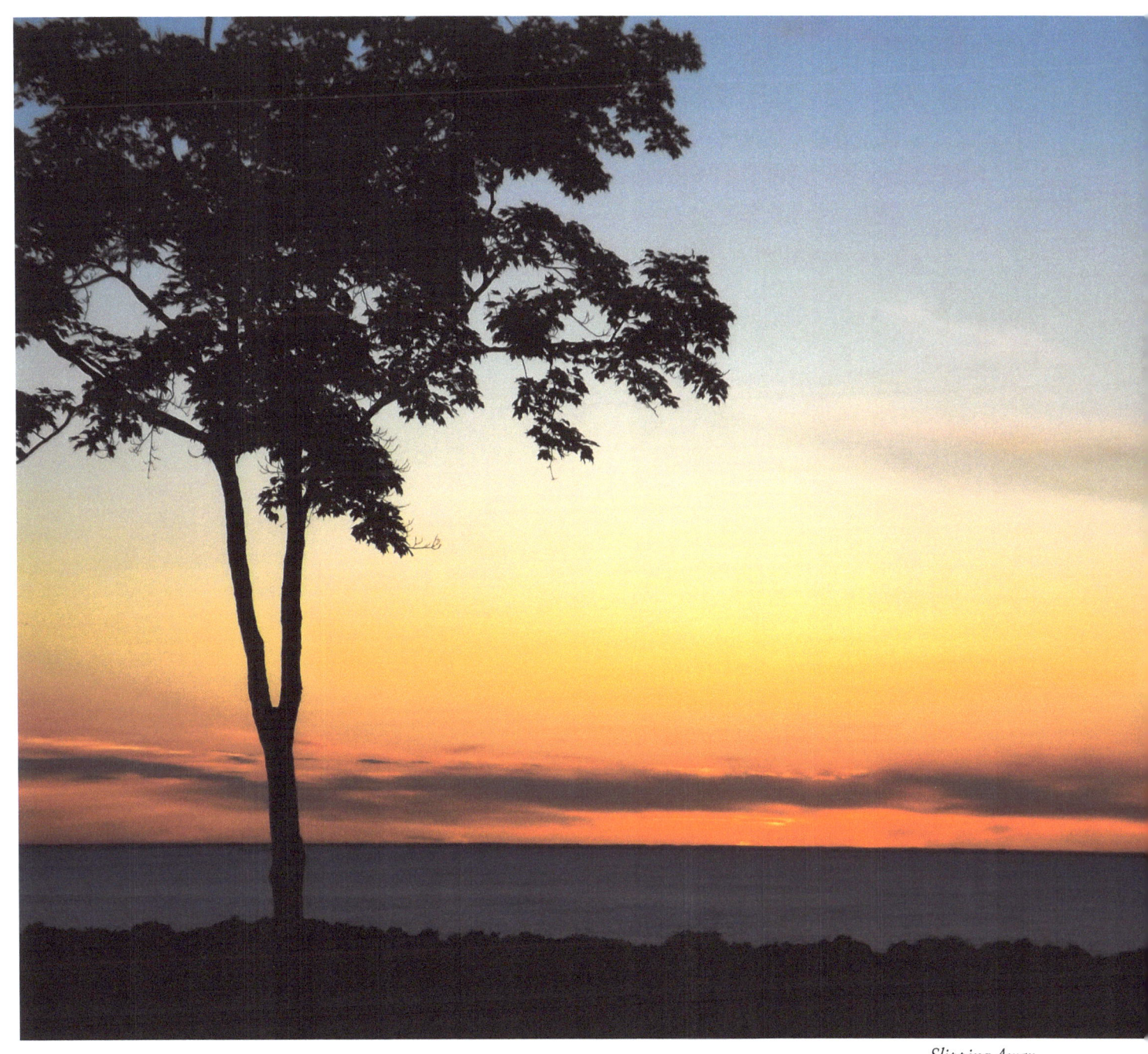

Slipping Away

Another day comes to an end as the sun slips away leaving beautiful colors behind a silhouetted tree.

The Pastels

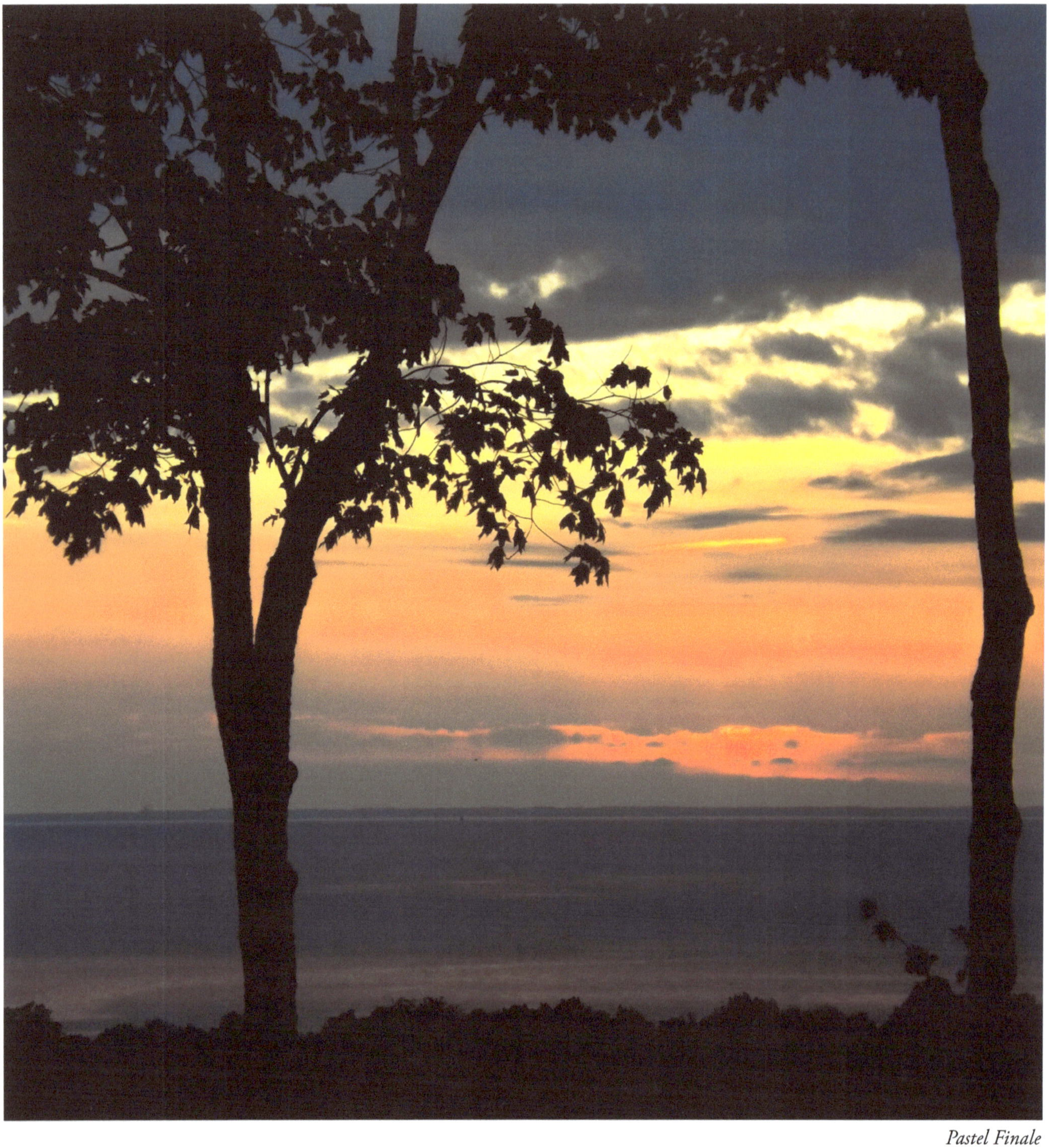

Pastel Finale

As the sun drops down beyond the horizon, the light fades to pastel hues of yellow, peach, and light blues.

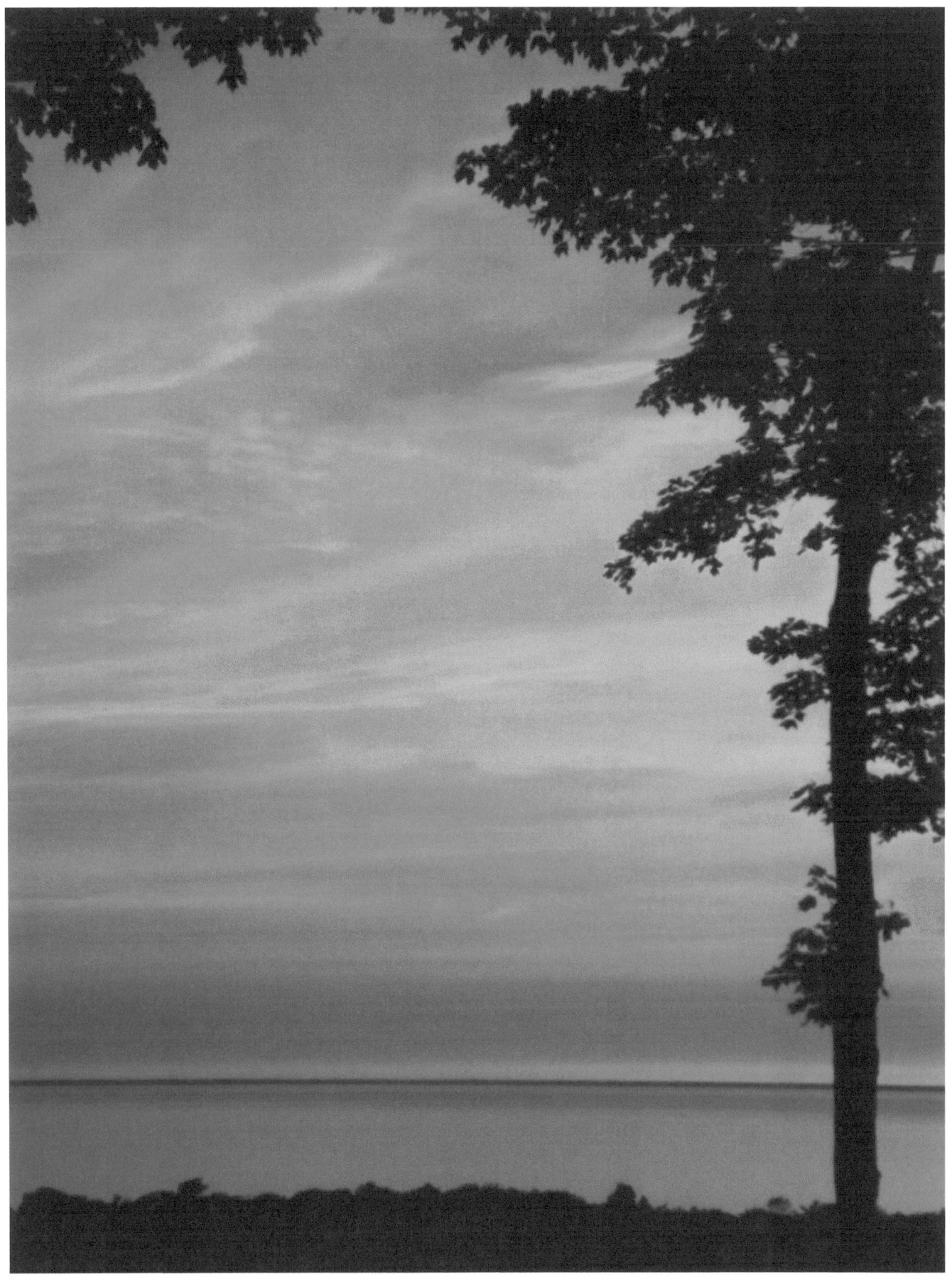

Peach Finale

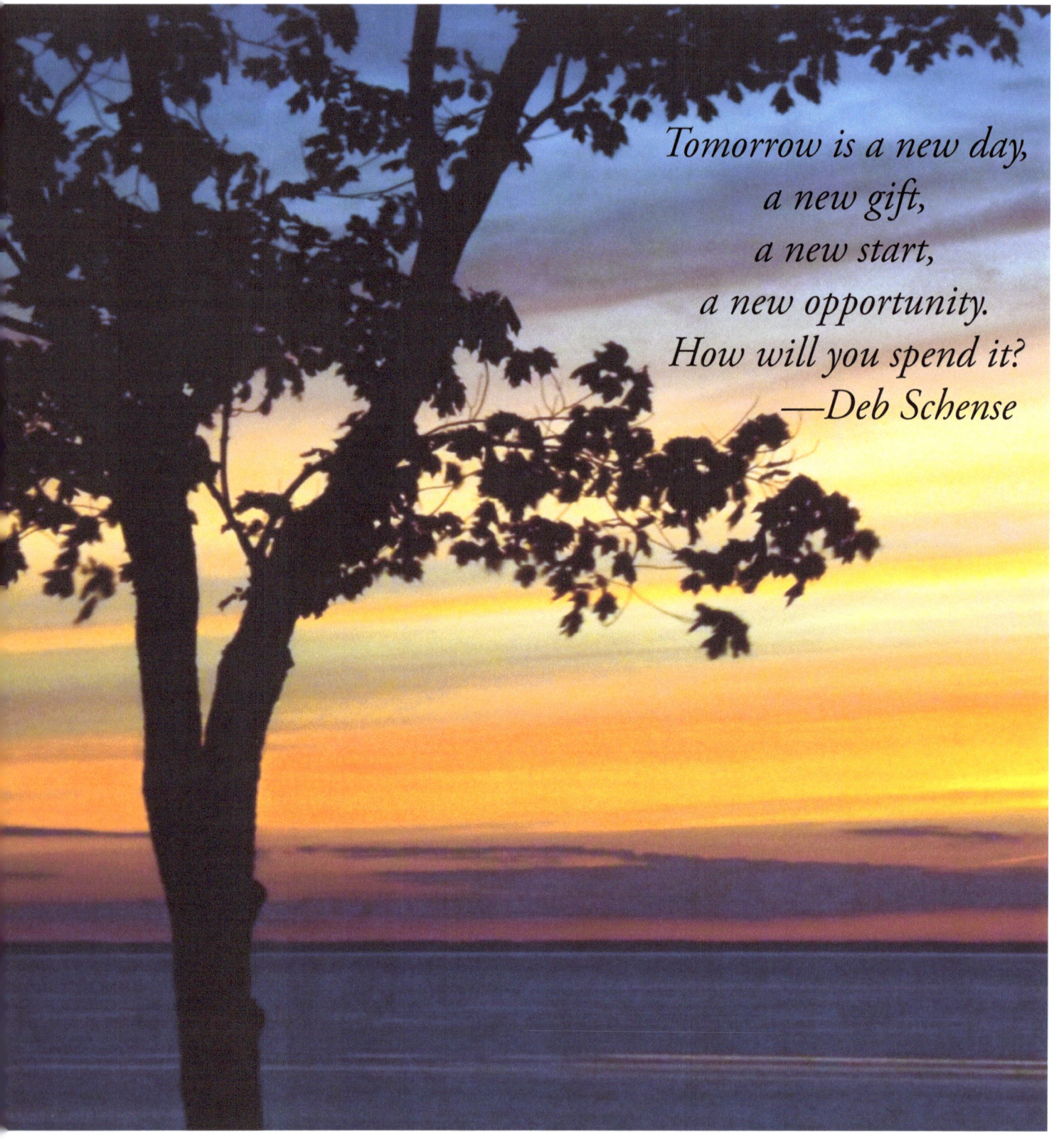

Tomorrow is a new day,
a new gift,
a new start,
a new opportunity.
How will you spend it?
—Deb Schense

Pastel Grande

If you enjoyed this book, please leave a review on www.amazon.com. To order prints, of any of the images in this book and other categories, please visit: http://deb-schense.artistwebsites.com/. For more information on books by the same author, please visit: debschense.wix.com/bookem. Greeting cards may be ordered individually or in quantities of twenty-five. For more information, contact the author at debschense@gmail.com.

www.ingramcontent.com/pod-product-compliance
Lightning Source LLC
Chambersburg PA
CBHW040747200526
45159CB00023B/1759